KING OF CANNES

KING OF CANNES

Madness, Mayhem, and the Movies

Stephen Walker

Algonquin Books of Chapel Hill   2000

Published by
Algonquin Books of Chapel Hill
Post Office Box 2225
Chapel Hill, North Carolina 27515-2225

a division of
Workman Publishing
708 Broadway
New York, New York 10003

First published in the United Kingdom by William Heinemann,
Random House UK Limited.
Printed in the United States of America.

Library of Congress Cataloging-in-Publication Data
Walker, Stephen, 1961–
    King of Cannes : madness, mayhem, and the movies / Stephen Walker.—1st ed.
      p.   cm.
    ISBN 1-56512-269-0
    1. Walker, Stephen, 1961—Diaries.   2. Motion picture producers and
directors—Great Britain—Diaries.   3. Cannes Film Festival—Anecdotes.
    I. Title.

PN1998.3.W342 A3   2000
791.43'0233'092—dc21   99-086953

10 9 8 7 6 5 4 3 2 1
First Edition

Acknowledgements

First, I must thank the film-makers who featured in my documentary. To Mike Hakata, James Merendino, Erick Zonca, Stephen Loyd, Gordon Mason and Spooky, all of whom showed patience, forbearing, and heroic amounts of tolerance every inch of the way. I must also acknowledge a debt of gratitude to everyone who made the film possible, to Hannah Berryman, Tessa Gogol, Brian Raftery, Bronwen Davies, to my producers Pascale Lamche, Christine Ruppert and James Mitchell at Littlebird, to my fantastically talented editors John Wilkinson and Chris King who got me out of so many holes, to the staff at First Class Post, to my brilliant cameramen Dave Bennett, Alan Doyle and Cian De Buitlear, and to all those many others who worked on the film and managed to put up with me for so long. Thanks also to my friends and colleagues at the BBC, in particular Stephen Lambert, Jane Hewertson and Alex Holmes. Also my terrific agents, Jane Villiers and Rachel Calder and all the staff at Tessa Sayle. My gratitude and love to them all. To my publishers Ravi Mirchandani and Andy McKillop. I owe everything for their advice and encouragement, and for taking a risk with my first book. The fact that I've survived at all, in a material sense, is entirely due to John Riordan, my ever-understanding bank manager. I must also thank Aaron Simpson and Frank Mannion, and all the many other film-makers from all over the world who graciously gave me their time and help. Above all, I owe everything to my wife Sally and daughter Kitty, for all the weeks and months they never saw me, and for the love they always give, uncritically, unsparingly and unconditionally, the greatest gift in the world.

FOR MY PARENTS

For their love, generosity and wisdom

Prologue

My grandfather used to tell a joke which went like this. Mr Plotnik, the circumcisor, bumps into Monty Fleischman in the street. Monty Fleischman is carrying a tiny baby in his arms. Mr Plotnik looks at the baby for a long, long time, he *appraises* the baby, and then he says, 'Monty Monty Monty, that's one beautiful baby boy you got there'. And Monty says, 'First, it's a girl not a boy, second let go of my finger.'

My story is a bit like that. Eighteen months ago I began work on a documentary film whose object was to follow four young, untried, untested, ambitious, impoverished and occasionally unhinged film-makers in their quest for fame and glory at the Cannes Film Festival. Like Mr Plotnik, I spent a long time looking for one thing and finding another. A long time looking for fantasies and finding reality. A long time looking for foreskins and finding fingers.

This is a record of that journey. It took me right into the underbelly of the movie business, a world whose existence up till then I had never suspected. I met literally hundreds of film-makers, in Britain, Ireland, France, Germany and the United States. Some of them were clearly talented. A number of them had absolutely no talent at all. A few of them were certifiably insane. What united them all was a passion for film-making and an almost inhuman deter- mination to make their mark — whatever the cost.

For all of these people the Cannes Film Festival was the great and overriding goal. To succeed at Cannes was to succeed like nowhere else. This was the jackpot, the lottery of lotteries. This was where half of Hollywood, and most of the world's media, gathered for two weeks every May. This was where Quentin Tarantino, the King of Low-Budget Underbelly Movie-Makers, had won the film world's most coveted movie prize, the *Palme d'Or* – and the world fell at his feet. This was the place whose mix of hype, decadence, sleaze, glamour, madness, power and sheer, unadulterated *glory* created an irresistible allure, and the promise of rewards to come. In the end, this was the Shrine. That, at least, was the fantasy. The reality was even more fantastic.

*   *   *

For as long as I can remember I had always wanted to go to the Cannes Film Festival. Each May, I gobbled up newspaper reports, gossip columns, film reviews. I too swallowed the Myth of Cannes. I wanted to go to the parties. I wanted to watch the movies. I wanted to see the stars. I wanted to climb the red-carpeted steps, all twenty-two of them, arm in arm with a gorgeous actress, caught in the glare of a hundred arc lights, a thousand cameras. This remained an unlikely ambition since (a) I wasn't a movie star, (b) I wasn't a famous director and (c) I wasn't a hotshot producer. On the other hand, if I couldn't take a film there, I could *make* a film there. All I had to do was persuade some gullible soul to stump up the necessary cash – preferably lots of it – and I was away. Simple as that.

At this point, the BBC came to the rescue. For the last ten years, I'd been working there, first as a researcher, then as a documentary director. I'd recently made a film about a Jewish wedding. It was a success. Then I made one about toys. It was a disaster. This put me in an interesting position on the cash-raising front. I was, in effect, a walking

4

oxymoron. A success/failure. Neither a sure bet nor a certain catastrophe. My strategy was clear: to find an unusual angle, to pitch it with panache, and — my joker in the pack — to appeal to the vanity of cash-rich executive producers in and out of the BBC. Conversations would go like this:

INT. OFFICE. DAY.

Executive Producer wearing Armani suit and no tie sits at desk drinking decaffeinated coffee out of a Wedgwood china cup. I sit opposite wearing jeans, sneakers and ancient T-shirt drinking tap water out of a plastic beaker.

> EXECUTIVE PRODUCER
> So. You've got five minutes. Make that four. No three. And it better be more interesting than that goddamn awful crap thing you did about toys. Shoot. Like I said — you got two minutes.

> ME
> It's about . . . Cannes.

> EXECUTIVE PRODUCER
> I don't do holiday shows.

> ME
> No, no. Cannes. The Film Festival. (*Pause*) In the South of France? (*Pause*) Near Nice?

> EXECUTIVE PRODUCER
> I'm not a fucking moron, you know, I know where Cannes is. It's near Nice.

> ME
> OK. So. It's . . . four guys. Directors. First-timers. They're crazy.

Impoverished. Obsessed. Ruthless. They'll sell their own grandmothers to get their movie made.

> EXECUTIVE PRODUCER.
> (*picking his teeth*)

So?

> ME

So . . . they go to Cannes. To the Film Festival. The biggest film festival in the world.

> EXECUTIVE PRODUCER
> (*examining his nails*)

So?

> ME

So . . . they go to . . . sell their movies. To make a splash. To hit the jackpot. To win the lottery of lotteries. It's . . . it's got *everything*. Tragedy. Comedy. Tragicomedy. Pathos. Disaster. Triumph Over the Odds. Sex. It's David and Goliath. It's . . . *The Full Monty* meets *Trainspotting*. It's *Titanic* meets . . .

> EXECUTIVE PRODUCER
> (*he interrupts*)

I fucking hated that movie.

> ME

Which movie?

> EXECUTIVE PRODUCER

All of them.

> ME
> (*time to play the joker*)

OK. I reckon I can get you invites for the Sharon Stone party, Bruce Willis's yacht party, Claudia Schiffer's Hotel Bedroom

Pyjama party, Demi Moore's Members Only Swingers Party at the Hotel du Cap, Robert Redford's . . .

EXECUTIVE PRODUCER
When do we start?

*   *   *

I suppose it was my mum who first got me interested in documentaries. I was brought up in a house of locked doors. The downstairs loo was always locked. The airing cupboard was always locked. The door to the living-room was always locked. If my mother was in the kitchen, she'd lock the door to her bedroom. Like Fort Knox, getting into my house meant negotiating a plethora of locks, bolts, hinges and alarms. To date, I'm not sure why my mother did this, although it may have been connected to her profound suspicion of cleaners. She was always convinced they were out to nick everything in the house (down to the toilet rolls). Her definition of a cleaner was basically a kleptomaniac who occasionally helped with the washing-up. At any rate, the result was that I became extremely interested in locked doors. I wanted to know what lay behind them. I wanted to know what secrets they contained. This left me with two options in life: either (a) to become a professional burglar, or (b) to become a documentary film-maker. I chose (b). With hindsight, I'm not sure there's much difference.

The great thing about documentary film-making is that it is a licence to spy. It's the definitive nosy-parker profession. When I joined the BBC ten years ago, I instantly found myself at home among a whole load of other nosy parkers, all of whom were actually getting paid for it. My very first job was to work on a series about the human body. By a curious coincidence, I got the nose. After several weeks' research, I found a woman who was able to play Beethoven's 'Moonlight Sonata' on the piano with her nose, a man who was in the *Guinness Book of Records* for the largest nose in Great Britain (it was six and a half inches long) and a man with the loudest snore in the world (like a car backfiring, only louder.)* It was my first experience of documentary film-making. It was, in fact, paradise.

Ten years and 22 films later, paradise was looking a little ragged. Too many late nights in edit suites or on location, too many blazing rows, panic attacks, sweating fits, crushing headaches, rushed deadlines, horrible nightmares, broken weekends, disastrous screenings, insane schedules, cardiac scares. It was time to move on. Time to rejuvenate the system. Time to inject a few billion volts of pure, adrenaline-pumping, movie-making *energy* into the job. And that's when, like manna from heaven, this film came along.

Here, at last, was an opportunity to rediscover the roots of film-making. To dig deep into the obsessions, the dreams, the ambitions, the madness which lurk in every film-maker, especially the sort of low-budget, low-rent, low-living film-makers I was going to meet. These were the sort of people who mortgaged their homes (if they had homes), ran up credit card debts of thousands of pounds, sold everything they'd ever owned, begged money off all their friends, in some cases virtually stopped eating, in order to fund their movies. They lived, breathed, slept, dreamt movies. Nothing else mattered. Nothing else was as important. Their role model was Roberto Rodriguez, a director crazy, or deter-mined, or desperate enough to volunteer as a guinea pig in a

---

* This is really true. Noise pollution officers sat up all night outside his house recording decibel levels.

8

series of medical experiments in order to raise $7000 for his first movie. The result, in his case, was *El Mariachi* and international stardom. Among the people I met the feeling was, if he can do it, *why not me?*

It was an eye-opener. Pretty well every film I'd ever seen about Cannes played from the perspective of the rich and famous, the movers and shakers of the industry. My film was going to be about the underdogs. I wanted the ant's eye perspective. The film-makers I met saw in Cannes the opportunity of a lifetime. Whether they were there to sell an idea, a script, or a movie, it didn't matter. The point was . . . *to do it.* To create an impact. To bang a few heads. To crash every party, haunt every bar, badger every miserable, beleaguered executive who happened to step out of his or her suite at the Carlton Hotel. To pitch in lobbies, lifts, cafés, streets, taxis, screenings, yachts, everywhere and anywhere they could. What emerged was a clash of tragicomic proportions between one bunch of cocooned, powerful, egomaniacal, occasionally corrupt Goliaths . . . and this other bunch of Davids: young, hungry, sharp as knives – and squatting on someone else's floor.

The Davids are the heroes of my story. The real Kings of Cannes.

April, 1999

ACT I

Pre-Production

FRIDAY, 2 JANUARY, LONDON

Last night I had dinner with a friend of mine who is a vet. He recently worked out he sticks his finger up an animal's bottom an average of five times a day. This equates to 25 times a week. Since he's been a vet for 19 years, this means he's stuck his finger up various animal bottoms approximately 23,750 times, not including overtime and allowing for two weeks' holiday a year. He said job satisfaction was beginning to be a bit of a problem.

I know how he feels.

Here I am, 36 years old, 23 films behind me. The 23rd — a film about toys — was a disaster. As far as I can gather, nobody watched it. My boss hated it. My editor thought it was incoherent. The critics panned it. My cameraman and I aren't talking. People sat stone-faced through all the screenings. I had fantasies of murdering the lot of them. Frankly, I'd rather be a vet.

And now, looming on the horizon, there's Cannes.

MONDAY, 5 JANUARY, LONDON

First day in the office. There are four of us. Hannah, my assistant producer, Pascale, my producer, and Bronwen, the production assistant. A quick round-up of each: Hannah, blonde, pretty, full of beans, raring to go, terrifyingly efficient. I figure I can let her do maybe 90 per cent of the work and claim all the glory. Pascale, thin, nervous, highly strung, very brittle (especially with me), a serious cinephile, given to spouting names of obscure directors/movies I've never heard of. I think this is designed to keep me in my place. Finally Bronwen. She is Welsh but for some reason best known to herself affects a French accent when on the phone. She and Pascale are thick as thieves, which means I spend a lot of time telling each how wonderful the other one is. The result is that neither of them trusts me one bit.

Cannes starts on 13 May. We've got 18 weeks. Or 128 days. Or 3073 hours. Or 184,320 minutes. Or 11,059,200 seconds. By that time we've got to have a cast lined up – three or four film-makers who can sustain a story through 90 minutes. Ninety minutes is a hell of a long time to sit down in front of a TV screen. *Titanic*, maybe. The World Cup Final, possibly. But a documentary? The awful, sickening, panic-inducing, heart-stopping thing about making a documentary is that *nobody knows what's going to happen*. Maybe nothing will happen. Maybe everything will happen. All I know is this: we need to cast the net as widely as possible. Find the best characters wherever we can, the funniest, the most out-spoken, the most outrageous, the most unhinged, the most daring, the ones who will kill their grannies to get their movie made or sold. And we have to find them fast.

WEDNESDAY, 7 JANUARY, LONDON

This office is a shambles. For one thing, it overlooks a building site. The din is terrific – bang bang bang all day long. For another, there's only one phone between four of us.

Last week I asked Bronwen, our secretary, when we might expect another phone.

'Tomorrow,' she says.

Next day, no phone.

'When's the phone coming?' I ask.

'End of the week,' she replies.

At the end of the week, no phone.

'Where's the phone?' I enquire.

'Next month,' she answers. 'It's the earliest they can do.'

I spend most of the time staring at the wall.

Meanwhile, Pascale and I are not seeing eye to eye. A large part of the finance for our film comes from Germany. This means there's a lot of pressure to put a German in it.

'We're going to have to put a German in the film,' says Pascale. 'Otherwise the Germans will pull all their money out.'

'But I don't want to put a German in it,' I reply. Everybody knows Germans are terminably boring.

'Everybody knows Germans are terminably boring,' I protest.

'I know,' says Pascale. 'But we won't have any money if we don't put one in it.'

This afternoon, I manage to bag the phone for three minutes. I call Roger Randall-Cutler, producer of *The Commitments*. He works above a sex shop in Soho. I once took an idea to him for a feature film set in the eighteenth century about an aristocratic dwarf who marries an Italian princess who also happens to be a dwarf and who together create a household full of dwarfs including a dwarf butler and a dwarf master of hounds who hunts rabbits with chihuahua dogs. Roger said he didn't think it was really his cup of tea.

Now I tell him all about the Cannes film. He tells me it

isn't really his cup of tea. Which is just as well because my three minutes are up and Bronwen wants to use the phone.

Everyone says that, what with the Lottery and everything, there's loads of money sloshing around the British film industry right now. But Hannah doesn't agree. She's been speaking to somebody who finally, after years of effort, achieved his lifelong ambition to make a film about Sigmund Freud. He did this by raising money from the Welsh Film Foundation. The only condition was that the entire film had to be in Welsh.

At this rate, our film is going to be entirely in German.

MONDAY, 12 JANUARY, LONDON

On the look-out for possible contenders, Hannah and I have decided to stick an ad in a number of newspapers. This is what we come up with:

> BBC TV seek crazy obsessive hungry shameless ruthlessly ambitious film-makers who are going to Cannes this year to sell their movie/script/selves and will kill their own grandmothers to do so. Please apply etc, etc.

Hannah is a bit worried we'll get a whole bunch of nutters calling in, but I'm prepared to take the risk – and anyway, she'll be taking the calls. The danger with this approach, tried and tested though it is, is that it's extremely unpredictable. There are millions of people out there with frighteningly inflated ideas about how interesting/crazy/obsessive/ruthless/shameless they actually are. (I know. I'm one of them.)

Last time I put an ad in the paper was two years ago, when I did my Jewish wedding film. A tiny notice went into the *Jewish Chronicle*. Within twenty-four hours my answerphone was jammed with 356 messages. 186 were from Jewish mothers who wanted their daughters to be on TV; 72 from Jewish mothers who wanted their daughters to be *in* TV; 97 from bona fide couples who wanted to know more (these included my doctor's daughter, the son of the man who owns my local deli, and the granddaughter of the man who fitted my Barmitzvah suit in 1974). There was also one from somebody who lived in Bolton, who said he got an erection from bursting balloons. He didn't say whether he was Jewish.

TUESDAY, 20 JANUARY, LONDON

This afternoon I meet a young producer from Northern Ireland, Michael Hughes. With his brother Enda, he has made a film called *Eliminator*. It cost £2000 and starred Michael, Enda and one of their cousins who lives down the road and who doubled up as stunt co-ordinator, clapper-loader, designer, chippie and lighting electrician. The end credit list runs for over six minutes with all of their names each appearing 87 times. *Eliminator* has the longest car chase in the history of cinema and the reason I know this is because Enda made a point of timing the length of every single car chase ever filmed and then making his exactly one minute longer. This is by any definition a remarkable achievement considering (a) the size of the budget and (b) the fact that none of the cars involved actually had an engine. They were towed by a tractor owned by another cousin who lives over in the next village. Apparently, he wants to get into the movies.

Michael himself is charming, articulate and ridiculously young. He says things like, 'After Oxford, I worked in the theatre as an actor, then studied in Paris for a year before producing my first feature film.' He is just 23. He first got into movies at the age of six when he and his brother borrowed their dad's Super 8 camera and did a spectacular remake of *Raiders of the Lost Ark* in their back garden. After that came the remake of *Indiana Jones and the Temple of Doom*, also in the back garden. While other kids in the neighbourhood were doing all the normal things kids do, Michael and Enda got on with the business of remaking the entire Spielberg *oeuvre* at a millionth of the cost. Then they built a cinema in the garage so their mum and dad could watch all their movies. Now they're being tipped as the next Tarantinos. More to the point, they're intending to go to Cannes.

Michael brings me up to date with his latest projects. There's *Flying Saucer Rock 'n' Roll*, in which a bunch of aliens invade South Armagh. There's also *Frock Cop*, about an RUC policeman in Northern Ireland who goes undercover as a secret agent and discovers in the process that he's actually a transvestite. 'It's a very serious film,' says Michael. 'As far as I am aware, nobody has ever confronted this particular aspect of the Troubles.'

Back at the office, Hannah fills me in about someone called Nick O'Riller, a young director who is going to Cannes to pitch his latest script, *Siamese Cop*. This is the story of two policemen (one good, one bad) who are joined at the hip. Apparently, Nick O'Riller is being tipped as the next Tarantino.

WEDNESDAY, 21 JANUARY, LONDON

I'm having problems with meetings. Every time I try to get a meeting with anybody vaguely important, they're always in a meeting. Conversations go like this:

INT. MY OFFICE. DAY.

I am on the only phone. For the next five minutes it is all mine. I dial the number of a well-known producer to set up a meeting.

ME

Good morning. Can I speak to (*name of well-known producer*).

SECRETARY'S VOICE

He's in a meeting.

ME

Oh. Well, can I speak to (*name of another well-known producer*).

SECRETARY'S VOICE

He's also in a meeting.

ME

Oh. When will he be free?

SECRETARY'S VOICE

I haven't a clue. But I know he's got another meeting after that. Then he's got a meeting with (*she mentions the first producer who's already in a meeting*) after he's finished his meeting. I'd put you through to his assistant but unfortunately she's in a meeting. A meeting meeting.

ME

A meeting meeting?

19

That's right. Otherwise I'd interrupt her. Tell you what. I'll get her to call you back. Say around two thirty?

I can't. I've got a meeting.

Whole days go by like this. As a result, while Cannes is getting closer, I'm getting nowhere.

THURSDAY, 29 JANUARY, LONDON

Amazingly, I manage to get a meeting with Derek Malcolm, esteemed film critic of the *Guardian*. He manages to say *'Clint'* about fifteen times in the first five minutes: 'Well of course I told Clint he ought to cut twenty minutes out of his movie ...' Then there's *'Marty'* and *'Kevin'* and *'Steven'*, and it takes me a minute or two to realize he's talking about Scorsese, Costner and Spielberg. He has bucket-loads of advice about what they all ought to cut from their movies. He's less specific about whether or not they took it.

Derek tells me about his life. He tells me how every year he goes to lots of film festivals. He goes to San Sebastian, to Jerusalem, to Sundance, to Venice, to Berlin, to New York, to Dublin, to Singapore and, of course, to Cannes. All his expenses are paid because he is such a famous film critic and (as we already know) on first-name terms with all the most famous directors and actors in the business. 'It's a tough life being a film critic,' he says. 'But someone has to do it.' And at least he gets to offer everyone the benefit of his advice.

Derek also describes the Byzantine system of accreditation which operates in Cannes. This is colour-coded and works at various levels. At the bottom is yellow, the lowest of the low which will get you just about nowhere but is, I suppose, better than no pass at all. Next, in ascending order, is blue, then pink, then pink with a yellow dot and, finally, white. White is for the *crème de la crème*, the most exclusive and coveted of all passes in Cannes. With a white pass you can do anything, go anywhere and, I believe, personally strike a policeman without fear of reprisal. Derek has a white pass. 'You have to be either Derek Malcolm or the Blessed Virgin Mary to get a white pass,' he says.

I ask him what sort of pass he thinks we'll get.

'Yellow,' he answers. 'Of course, you'll be right at the bottom of the whole pile.'

I make a mental note that, should Derek Malcolm ever be in the unlikely position of offering me advice about any movie I make, I'll make sure it stays right at the bottom of the pile.

Friday, 30 January, London

Our phone machine is jammed with messages. Hannah says one of them was from a man who gets an erection from bursting balloons. I ask whether he's from Bolton and she spends the rest of the morning giving me curious looks.

Lunch with Michael Hurst, a film-maker from Brighton. He already has one feature film, *Project Assassin*, to his credit. He hands me the script for his next, *New Blood*, for which (he says) he has raised $2m and which starts shooting in March. Meanwhile, he is hard at work on his third script. He is 22 years old.

Michael's idea of a good time is to watch three or four movies a day (when he's not making them). Most of these are

B movies with titles like *Star Crash* (an Italian rock-bottom budget rip-off of *Star Wars*). Michael says you haven't lived until you've seen *Star Crash*.

He also tells me about somebody called Lloyd Kaufman – apparently a sort of Goliath in the B (and C and D) movie world. Kaufman lives in New York and produces films like *Toxic Avenger* (the story of a man who falls into a vat of nuclear acid and becomes a superhero). Michael says you haven't lived until you've seen *Toxic Avenger*.

Later, I watch *Project Assassin*. It's incredibly violent. I read the script of *New Blood*. It's even more violent. I'm a bit worried about Michael. I mean, he's a nice guy and all that but . . . what if he gets cross with me? I might end up in a vat of nuclear acid.

A visit to my hairdresser this afternoon. He tells a joke which goes like this: a little Jewish man in his eighties gets into a lift when the most stunning woman you ever saw follows him in. Blonde and beautiful, she is the ultimate male fantasy. The lift doors close and the woman winks at the little Jewish man and then she says, 'You know it's always been my fantasy to be in a lift like this with an older man and go down on my knees and open his flies and give him the most incredible blow-job he's ever had in his entire life.' And the little Jewish man says, 'That's all very well. But what's in it for me?'

This cheers me up no end and more than compensates for the fact that each time I visit my hairdresser he has less hair to cut. Moreover, I have definitely noticed that my hair is starting to go grey since I began working on this film (two weeks ago). At this rate I will be dead before I am finished with it.

Wednesday, 4 February, London

Chaos still reigns in the office. Every phone conversation is punctuated by the sound of drilling, hammering, thwacking, yelling, banging and slamming from the builders next door. The net result is we spend all day screaming down the phone like a bunch of drill sergeants. Everyone we speak to thinks we are either insane or completely deaf. Yesterday, Pascale suddenly hurled the phone on the floor yelling, 'I CAN'T TAKE IT ANY MORE!' This wasn't a sensible thing to do since it's the only phone we've got. At least now we don't have to talk to anybody. As for Pascale, I notice she's losing her voice. Apparently, we are going to have some double-glazing installed, which means more drilling, this time from the inside.

This evening, a man arrives in the office while I am busy staring at the wall. I think he's come about the double-glazing since he seems particularly interested in the windows but in fact he turns out to be my boss. I've only met him once before. Now he's come to say hello. I say hello back. He tells me how incredibly excited he is about our film, which is a complete surprise to me since so far we don't actually *have* a film – i.e. no stories, no characters and no access. He also says he has great hopes the film will première at the Sundance Film Festival next year. This is going to cause me several sleepless nights. Sundance is *the* US showcase for independent movies. Half of Hollywood turns up in force. You can make or break your career at Sundance. I have visions of breaking mine in spectacular style.

Later, I get a fax from Andrea, our German researcher. She is busy trying to find interesting German film-makers for us. It seems to me that after three weeks' research there aren't any interesting German film-makers, only boring ones, but that perhaps having a boring German film-maker might actually be quite interesting. She describes one film-maker called Stefan Juergens who is currently working on his latest film, *Airbag Generation*, about a woman who has her breasts enlarged thirteen times. Opinion in Germany is divided as to whether or not Stefan Juergens is the next Orson Welles. I am to meet him later this month.

TUESDAY, 10 FEBRUARY, LONDON

I'm seriously thinking of sticking up a great big chart on the wall with all my favourite A list, B list and C list name droppers on it. Right up there on the A list (along with Derek Malcolm) is Charles Finch, a big cheese at the William Morris Agency in London. Today, I visit him at the Twentieth Century Fox Building in Soho Square. In his early forties, Charles Finch sits in his office and sticks his feet up on the desk. I *hate* it when people do that. It makes me want to do the same thing, i.e. stick my feet up on *his* desk. But I don't. Instead, I sit upright and listen while Charles drops famous names all over the carpet. We get *'Francis'* three times within the first fifteen seconds and it takes me a minute or two to realise he's talking about Francis Ford Coppola, by which time he's on to *'Bobby'* (that's Robert to me and you) De Niro, *'Demi'* (Moore), *'Jack'* (Nicholson), *'Ridley'* (Scott) and another *'Bobby'* (Duvall). Pausing briefly for breath, he says: 'So what's your name again?'
'Stephen.'
'Is that Steven as in Spielberg or with a ph?'
'With a ph.'
'Got it,' he says. 'As in Stephen Frears.'
The thing about people like Charles Finch (that's *'Charlie'*

to his friends) is that I don't know half or even three-quarters of the names they drop. I'm OK with big actors (Bobby De Niro) or big directors (Steven Spielberg) but when it comes down to the nitty gritty of the movie business I'm lost. Charles, on the other hand, bulldozes his way enthusiastically through trunk-loads of sales agents, PR people, producers, distributors, film lawyers, executives, financiers and exhibitors without pausing for breath. It is obvious my role is to sit there and be impressed but it is difficult to be impressed when (a) I am bored to the point of rigor mortis and (b) all I can see of Charles from where I sit are his shoes.

Charles says that the key person in his agency – 'the guy you just *have* to meet' – is somebody called Cassian.

Cassian turns out to be Cassian Elwes, which is rather remarkable because I actually know who he is. In fact, I've met him before. Back in 1995, I was in Los Angeles, trying unsuccessfully to raise money for a television drama starring John (Hurt). John (Hurt) gave me a few names and that's how, one smoggy morning, I got to meet Cassian (Elwes) for breakfast.

The first mistake I made was the hotel itself. Nobody told me that where you stay in LA is who you are. I was staying at the cheapest place in town, the Howard Johnson Motel miles away from anywhere. They did a very good Bargain Break for $45 a night plus tax. This also included breakfast, which is what I was having when Cassian (Elwes) turned up with one of his associates. In a Porsche.

The associate said, 'Where the fuck did you find *this* place?'

Before I had a chance to tell him all about the Bargain Break for $45 a night plus tax, he was yelling into his mobile phone. 'I said *ten fucking million and no less!* That's what (*names huge mega star*) costs. Whaddya think this is, a fucking *charity*?'

And to me: 'Wouldn't *you* pay ten million for (*names huge mega star again*)?'

'Well,' I said, 'to be absolutely honest, I haven't ever —'

'He's an expensive sonafabitch but he's worth it. So what's your movie?'

My second mistake was to order the wrong kind of breakfast. I didn't realise that what you eat in Los Angeles is what you are. The best thing to do is eat nothing at all. If you're feeling really hungry, maybe have a little freshly squeezed organic mango juice. I had the Hungry Pioneers Hearty Breakfast Special, which was bacon, sausage, tomato, hash browns, three eggs sunny side up, toast, butter, coffee, full-cream milk and your choice of cereal. Cassian and his associate ordered the mango juice.

Then I told him all about the film.

'It's scheduled to go out on the fiftieth anniversary of the war.'

'What war?'

'The Second World War,' I said.

'That was fifty years ago?'

'Yes,' I said.

'Well,' said the associate, 'I'll be damned. So what's the story?'

Between mouthfuls of bacon, egg, toast, hash browns, sausage and tomato, I told them the story. All this time, Cassian said nothing. He began to look bored. Then he looked out of the window. Then he looked at his watch. Then he looked at his mobile phone, as if willing it to ring. Then he yawned. Then he said, 'You've got a piece of sausage on your face.'

It was the only thing he said and it has to be one of the most brilliant pieces of one-upmanship I have ever come across. It stopped me dead in my tracks. My pitch was over, dead in the water, finished, *kaput*. In the end, the film got made, but not thanks to Cassian Elwes and the William Morris Agency.

And now, here I am, three years later, and it looks as if we might be about to renew our acquaintance.

Wednesday, 11 February, London

Hannah has been speaking to a man called Graham Simmonds, a semi-retired businessman who lives on the Isle of Man. At the age of sixty, he has decided to fulfil a lifelong ambition and become a film producer. Despite knowing nothing about the movie business, he has half a million quid to blow. This makes him, in the UK at least, something of a player. His only conditions are (1) that the film has to be set in the Isle of Man, (2) that it has to have a strong love interest and (3) that it has to employ only local talent. The last stipulation is proving a bit of a problem since, after several months' research, he's discovered there isn't any local talent. Graham has a funny way of talking, like a cross between a tax inspector and the Queen. He says, 'We are told by those who have knowledge of such matters that the Cannes Film Festival is an opportunity to establish business connections with due diligence.'

'Sorry?' says Hannah.

She asks him how he got into movies.

'We wanted to develop a business in which we could foster the more indulgent sides to our nature,' he says.

'Who's we?' says Hannah.

'Me,' says Graham.

Despite knowing nothing about movies, Graham does know what he likes. In fact, he has a pretty good idea already of the kind of film on which he wants to spend his half-million. The particular story he has in mind seems to involve a millionaire businessman who comes to the Isle of Man and falls in love with a gorgeous, young female. They get up to all sorts of shenanigans in the wild and picturesque landscape of the Isle of Man – thus satisfying conditions (1) and (2) – but Graham is not quite sure how it ought to end. He has plenty of ideas as to who might play the female lead (Sharon Stone, Julie Walters, Demi Moore?) but has so far not come up with a single suggestion as to who might play the millionaire businessman.

'I know,' says Hannah. 'Why don't you play him yourself?'

'I never thought of that,' says Graham.

What makes Graham interesting from our point of view is that he intends to take his idea to Cannes. This offers tragicomic potential as he'd be just about the most unlikely person who ever went to Cannes since the Festival began in 1947. In a world which prides itself on its glamour, its glitter and its cool, I'd say Graham Simmonds stands apart. But he does have half a million quid. The prospect of Graham being dumped in the middle of the Cannes shark pool opens a whole new dimension to our film. Will he be ripped to pieces? Will he show them all a thing or two? Will Sharon Stone do the picture? Or will he get to foster the more indulgent sides to his nature? I ought to meet him.

I've been told that every morning at dawn during the Festival a giant dump truck goes up and down the sea front scooping up hundreds and thousands of unread scripts left lying in dustbins and on the street. All those hopes and dreams churned into shreds as the sun comes up over the city – a telling image.

FRIDAY, 13 FEBRUARY, LONDON

This evening I attend a lecture given by the New Producers Alliance, an organisation dedicated to foster the ambitions of young, untried film-makers. Some of their members will be going to Cannes to raise money for their pet projects, which is why the NPA run what they call a Cannes Survival Seminar. From what I can gather, this boils down to advice on where to get free booze (the British Pavilion), how to crash the best parties (pretend you're Robert De Niro's brother) and where to stay (on a camp site). The camp site is where everybody who is nobody in the movie business stays (i.e. probably 99 per cent of the membership of the NPA) since it only costs two quid a night compared with, say, two thousand quid a night at the Hotel du Cap (which is where everybody who is somebody in the movie business stays). For these reasons the NPA offers fertile ground for research. Which is why I'm here tonight.

The seminar takes place at the Royal College of Art. I arrive to find a lively party in full swing, champagne flowing, waiters carrying around goodies on trays, little knots of beautiful people in animated conversation. I wonder whether this is a dress rehearsal for the kind of party the NPA teach their members how to crash. After several glasses of champagne, it becomes clear that we are, in fact, in the wrong place. The NPA seminar is actually downstairs, in the basement, in a grubby lecture hall. Instead of champagne, there are a couple of bottles of warm fizzy water, and a bunch of people in old overcoats balancing notepads on their knees. A woman introduces the panellists, one of whom is an ex-BBC script editor I know. She has just made her first feature film. She tells a story about her initial encounter with an executive producer at the studio which was backing the film. He told her she was absolutely the perfect choice for director except he wasn't sure she had enough *edge*. The conversation went like this:

INT. EXECUTIVE PRODUCER'S OFFICE. DAY.

EXECUTIVE PRODUCER
We're not sure you've got enough edge.

MY FRIEND
Edge?

EXECUTIVE PRODUCER
Edge.

MY FRIEND
What's edge?

EXECUTIVE PRODUCER
What's edge? Edge is . . . You know . . . edge is . . . *edge*.

MY FRIEND
Edge?

EXECUTIVE PRODUCER
Exactly! Like . . . Quentin Tarantino has edge. Spike Lee has edge. Martin Scorsese has edge. *Edge*. Edge is what we need and we don't think you've got any.

(*Beat*)

Otherwise you're perfect.

So my friend went back to her office, took every single rape and murder scene she'd ever directed and stuck them all together in one seamless sequence of unparalleled brutality. Then she sent it off to the studio. Nobody ever mentioned edge again.

After a couple of hours I leave. I feel somehow fraudulent being there, on the sidelines, observing, deciding whether this person or that will make good material for my film. Both the awful and wonderful things about documentary making are the ability to drop into people's lives at a moment's notice, charm them, trespass on their emotions and then stick the whole thing up on display for the world to see. The truth is, most of the people in this room don't have films to make, or money to make them and many of them never will. Such grand ideas as I have about my story – pitting David against Goliath – seem cheap in the presence of so many real-life Davids. That distance between the panel and the audience can be measured in inches. But in reality it's a universe apart, a chasm which very few ever manage to cross.

As for me, I fall asleep wondering if I have any edge.

Monday, 16 February, London

Over the past week I've been reading all about the Cannes Film Festival. Despite the fact that half a million pounds has been raised in order to make this film, I still don't have a clue what the Festival actually *is*. I haven't admitted this to my employers because if I do they will either pull all their money out or fire me. In the meantime, I have been trying to make sense of the whole thing. These are my notes:

First, there's the Market. The Market is just that – a place where movies are bought and sold. Every cinema screen in Cannes is booked solid months before the Festival by producers who want to present their movies to the industry. Approximately 600 movies get shown this way. The screenings are almost exclusively limited to buyers who either buy them, or try to buy them, or tell everybody else they are awful. Often they tell everybody else they are awful so they can buy them for a knock-down price. The whole thing soon turns into a giant poker game with the result that awful films get sold for vast sums of money and terrific films don't get sold at all.

The average buyer will go to ten movies a day. This doesn't mean they watch the whole movie. Typically, they'll stay for five minutes. If they love the movie, they leave because they want to strike a deal before the rest of the competition is half-way through their popcorn. If they hate it, they leave anyway. As a result, everybody leaves the movie within the first five minutes except the director, who sits all alone in an empty cinema and thinks absolutely everybody hated it. This is why buyers have a fantastic time in Cannes and directors – if they are mad enough to go there in the first place – all want to commit suicide.

That's the Market.

Then there's the Festival. This is actually quite separate from the Market, although the two events run side by side and have done so for years The Festival is hideously complicated. Many regard it as a Gallic plot deliberately designed to confuse all foreigners and ensure that the French walk off with all the prizes. I am still trying to work it out. As follows:

The Festival is made up of all the movies selected by various committees for special presentation except for those that are already being shown in the Market and are therefore not selected by anybody. The Festival is divided into several sections. These include Directors Fortnight (which presents mostly, but not always, the work of first-time directors), Critics Week (which presents movies selected by a body of French critics and which *may* sometimes — but not always — include the work of first-time directors who are not also in Directors Fortnight), Cinéma En France (which presents only French movies) and the German Forum (which presents only German movies except sometimes those movies which may *look* German but are in fact financed by non-Germans ... like the French).

Finally, at the top of the heap, there is the Official Selection. This is itself further subdivided into Un Certain Regard (where the stars walk up a blue carpet) and the Official Competition (where they walk up a red carpet). The Official Competition also shows movies which are Out of Competition. If you're Out of Competition, you can't compete for any of the prizes open to those movies which are In Competition but you still get the red carpet. If you're In Competition you can't compete for any of the prizes in any of the other sections of the Festival (e.g. Directors Fortnight, Critics Week etc.) since none of these sections actually offer prizes, except that any first-time director in any of these sections *may* compete for the *Camera d'Or*, which is itself often confused with the *Palme d'Or*, which is actually a different prize completely for which only films In Competition are in fact eligible.

Some people find all this a bit confusing, which is why they choose to show their films at the Berlin Film Festival instead.

WEDNESDAY, 18 FEBRUARY, BERLIN, 11.30 P.M.

Too exhausted to write. Also, I've managed to lose a lit cigarette in my bed, which means the hotel may burn down at any moment.

I'm here for the Berlin Film Festival. In part as a dry run for Cannes, in part to see if we can find any German film-maker to include in our project. Our German backers are getting itchy and want results.

My researcher, Andrea, lines up a whole heap of directors for me to meet. We see one of them this afternoon. His name is Alex Jovi, a young film-maker who speaks perfect American and looks like a Californian surfer. Since I am rapidly going bald and have put on nearly half a stone in the past two weeks, this instantly prejudices me against him. I make a mental note that even if everybody in the film is bound to be younger than me, they will definitely have to be fatter and uglier.

Alex has already been to Cannes once and gives me a detailed list of all the girls he slept with there. This takes about three hours. Now he is in Berlin and so far hasn't slept with anybody. He says Berlin is a crap festival. He gives me his card and says he'd be happy to be in our film and his agent will be calling to discuss his fee. I say we'll be in touch and manage somehow to lose his card on the way to the toilet.

I've been going to the toilet a lot, recently. I seem to have developed chronic constipation. My bowels are in knots. I'm sure this is a sign of stress. There are 74 days left till Cannes and everything is going horribly wrong. I have no cast, I have no story and I am rapidly running out of ideas. I am convinced this film will be a disaster of epic proportions.

My only hope is to get a doctor's certificate so they will release me from my contract. Meanwhile I sit for hours on the toilet and fantasise about getting run over.

THURSDAY, 19 FEBRUARY, BERLIN

Andrea drags me over to the Cinecentre, a grey Sixties block which is the heart of the Berlin Film Festival. It looks exactly like the Shepherd's Bush Shopping Centre and is about as glamorous. Arranged over three floors, it's stuffed to the gills with sales reps quaffing cheap Asti Spumante and wolfing stale sandwiches. The whole thing looks like it's been sponsored by British Rail. People wander about, buying and selling movies like tins of dog food. I begin to panic about Cannes. Will it be like this?

Later, we drive to East Berlin to meet Rolf-Peter Kahl. He is a young German director who has just finished his first feature, *Angel Express*. Andrea chats away in the taxi but all I do is watch in wonder as we drive swiftly through the Brandenburg Gate, from West to East Berlin. The last time I was here was in 1989, just as the Wall came down. Somebody hauled me up to stand on top of it. I remember looking down on the area of ground between this part of the Wall and the Brandenburg Gate itself, a no man's land formerly packed with gun emplacements, slit trenches, electric fences, razor-wire and border posts. Now, as far as the eye could see, it was littered with thousands of empty champagne bottles. It was a sight I will never forget and I think of it today, as the traffic lights turn from red to green and we speed across this ghost of a border.

Rolf-Peter Kahl is very charming and invites us to a screening of another film later this evening in which he plays the lead. The cinema is half empty and I feel for him; but he has already disappeared, too terrified to watch it. I can see his point, since the film begins with a five-minute shot of Rolf-Peter dancing stark-naked in a room dominated by a giant photograph of himself. This is a kind of egomaniacal onanism I can only guess at, except I don't have to since the film ends with a five-minute shot of Rolf-Peter vigorously masturbating over a picture of his ex-girlfriend in front of the mirror.

Afterwards, Rolf-Peter Kahl asks me whether I liked the movie.

'Fantastic,' I say.

'For me it is a journey of self-expression,' he says.

'Oh, absolutely.'

But I don't offer to shake his hand.

Friday, 20 February, Berlin

In driving sleet we take a taxi to meet Martin Walz, the director of a film called *Killer Condom.* This is about a giant condom which has extremely sharp teeth and goes around biting off people's penises. Martin looks like a fairly normal sort of guy but this is obviously an illusion, since anybody who spends six years raising the money to make a film about a condom which goes around biting off people's penises is clearly insane and should never be allowed anywhere near a camera. But this is Germany and the film has been a huge success. In the process, Martin has become a feminist icon and his film plays to wild applause at women's film festivals all over the world.

He shows me a poster for the film. It says THE RUBBER WHICH RUBS YOU OUT!!! and underneath is a picture which looks like a cross between an ad for Mates and the poster for *Jaws*. The condom really does have teeth and there are bits of something soft and fleshy stuck between them.

'The special effects were the most difficult,' says Martin. 'I am very lucky with my special-effects man who likes the idea of the film very much and I think he does a very good job, especially with the castration scenes.'

'Oh, right,' I nod.

'You know it is really a very simple story and full of clichés,' says Martin proudly.

Martin took *Killer Condom* to Cannes last year, where it created something of a sensation, not least because an actor went up and down the Croisette dressed as a condom with teeth. A friend of mine at university once did something a bit similar. He was invited to a party with the dress code 'period' and turned up as a used Tampax. He was also arrested by the police, whereas the actor who dressed up as a condom was mobbed everywhere and asked for his autograph (not an easy thing to do in the circumstances). *Killer Condom* was a huge success and immediately picked up for distribution by Lloyd Kaufman, the notorious B movie producer whose latest hits include *Stuff Stephanie in the Incinerator* and *Class of Nuke 'Em High*. As a result, Martin is now flush with money and ready to embark on his next film, which is about the life and times of Jesus. Unfortunately, it won't be ready in time for Cannes.

Back at the hotel in the afternoon to meet Stefan Juergens, the director of *Airbag Generation*, the film about the woman who has thirteen operations to enlarge her breasts. He is very tall and very thin, and speaks appalling English with terrific confidence. It transpires that *Airbag Generation* has not actually been made. At the moment, Stefan is just finishing the script and sorting out the cast. This obviously includes the lead actress whose breasts actually *have* been enlarged thirteen times. She's also had operations on her nose, her chin, her legs, her stomach and her lips. As a result, her lips now look like the inner tubing of a bicycle tyre. And her breasts are absolutely *huge*, like giant footballs. An average-sized male like myself could easily get lost in them.

'She has the biggest bosoms in Europe,' says Stefan. 'They are also the fourth biggest in the world. Each bosom weighs over six kilos.'

'They do?' I ask. 'How do they weigh them?'

Stefan never satisfactorily answers this. Instead, he says, 'Many men are erected when they see her. But me, I am interested in less titted girls. For me she is like . . . a sister.' He shows me a photograph. She's not at all like my sister. I ask why she had them done.

'I think when she was a little girl she has very small bosoms indeed and her mother and sister make fun with her. So she decides to make them bigger.'

Yes, but *six kilos*?

'You know under these bosoms she has a very good heart,' observes Stefan.

Stefan is about to shoot a trailer for *Airbag Generation*, which he intends to take to Cannes along with his star. It features the final scene of the film in which the actress is killed because her manager accidentally drops her on the floor. This raises two questions: (i) why six kilos of silicone are not enough to break the fall and (ii) why the manager should be carrying her around in the first place (I'd have thought it was asking for trouble). Before I leave, Stefan offers me some publicity material but I decline. I'm worried I'll get stopped at Heathrow.

Later, in bed, I have a series of identical dreams in which

I go into hospital for an operation on my breasts, only to be eaten by a giant condom.

Could this be a sign?

SATURDAY, 21 FEBRUARY, BERLIN

I spend the morning at the Cinecentre on the look-out for Eastern European film-makers who might be going to Cannes. I have this idea it could be interesting to follow someone from somewhere like Estonia who doesn't speak a word of anything except Estonian and who's trying to sell a film which is both hopelessly uncommercial and completely unintelligible. Amazingly, I find a stand marked ESTONIAN FILM FOUNDATION. Behind it is a man who is a dead ringer for Rasputin but in fact turns out to be the Estonian version of David Puttnam. Unfortunately, he doesn't speak a word of English. My Estonian isn't that good either, but we manage to find an interpreter who speaks Russian. I ask whether there are any Estonian films going to Cannes this year. His response is to collapse into uncontrollable hysterics until he finally falls off his chair. The interpreter translates this as 'No'.

After this I try the Russian stand. I ask a woman called Raissa who speaks impeccable English whether there are any Russian films going to Cannes this year.

'All Russian film-makers are monsters,' she says.

Back at the hotel, Andrea introduces me to Peter Lichtenfeld, a director who has just made a film about the Twenty-First International Trainspotting Competition in Helsinki. Since most of what I know about trains comes from *Thomas the Tank Engine*, we quickly run out of things to say.

Go to bed feeling sick and tired. Tomorrow is my last full

day in Berlin. What have I achieved here? My mind reels with bits and pieces of everyone's movies all running together in one blurred, confusing heap. I am beginning to lose sight of what my film is supposed to be about. All I know is that the Germans are threatening to pull out unless I can find a German to put in it. I suppose they see my film as some sort of positive advertisement for German cinema. Some advertisement. Trainspotters, porno musicals, killer condoms, women with giant breasts . . . Of them all, maybe Stefan Juergens is the most promising. At least he's going to Cannes. And he's funny. God knows whether *Airbag Generation* is a positive advertisement for German cinema. But right now it's all I've got.

SUNDAY, 22 FEBRUARY, BERLIN

Wake up to the phone ringing by my bed. It's Stefan Juergens. He asks if I want the good news or the bad news first. The good news, I say. He says the good news is that he has just persuaded Arnold Schwarzenegger and Pamela Anderson to be in his film. That's very good news, I say. Well, he says, to be totally honest it's not exactly Arnold Schwarzenegger and Pamela Anderson but an actor and an actress who look exactly like them. In fact, he continues, it's impossible to tell the difference. That's the bad news, I say. No, says Stefan. The bad news is that the lead actress has pulled out of the film.

So that's that, then.

My last meeting is with Hans Horn. He is one of the directors I was thinking of when I thought it might be quite interesting to put a very boring German in our film. He is enormously tall and wears a pair of wraparound sunglasses

40

even though it's night-time. He has just returned from Namibia where he's been researching a film about Jesus. After half an hour it turns out it isn't really Jesus at all but a sort of clone of Jesus. There's also a Joseph and Mary, except it turns out they aren't in fact Joseph and Mary but sort of robots who just look like them. Somewhere around this point I nod off. When I wake up, Hans Horn is still half-way through his film. Either he's so engrossed in his story or he can't see a thing through his sunglasses but in any case he doesn't seem to notice. It takes him three hours to finish. He says, 'It's just one of several ideas I'm working on. Maybe you will like to hear the others?'

'Another time,' I say.

Putting somebody like Hans Horn in the documentary is very tempting. The only danger is that it could backfire horribly with the result that my film could end up being even more boring than his.

TUESDAY, 24 FEBRUARY, LONDON

I am currently reading Joseph Goebbels's diary for 1945, which is proving a useful accompaniment to my ever increasing bouts of constipation. I have just got to the bit where Goebbels is sitting in the bunker, with the Russians closing in from all sides. The sky is filled with the roar and flash of artillery. The Americans and British are bombing Germany to smithereens. Disaster looms, the end is in sight, and Goebbels and his wife are busy planning suicide along with the murder of their six children.

I know how he feels.

Eleven weeks left and so far I have found – nobody. Hannah and I have scoured the length and breadth of Britain and Germany for one decent, funny, outrageous, obsessive, charismatic, crazy, ruthless film-maker. I have staked everything on this – my career, my reputation and half a million quid (admittedly of someone else's money). The result is a total blank. Nothing. Zero. The film I have in my head is clearly a total fantasy. It doesn't exist. Almost all the people I have met are abandoned in the middle of some private, never-to-be-realised dream of success and glory. Or they're not going to Cannes. Or both.

Thursday, 26 February, London

I get a call at the office from Michaela Harding, star of my film about the Jewish wedding. She fills me in with bits of news about her family. I remember how unsure I was about her story at the time – and yet in the end the film worked. Maybe I should trust my instincts a little more. She puts me on to Colin, her dad, whom I haven't spoken to for over a year. When I last saw him he was eighteen stone and desperately trying to lose weight in time for the wedding. He even bought an exercise machine. Now the exercise machine is in the attic and Colin is twenty-four stone. He tells me he's going to America to have a balloon inserted into his stomach. Apparently, this stops him wanting to eat so much, which means he'll probably weigh about eight stone when I next speak to him. He's very excited about the balloon and says I ought to make a film about it. Access is guaranteed and we can even stick a mini video camera on the end of the balloon when they put it in his stomach. 'You won't get more fly-on-the-wall than that,' says Colin.

So I suppose all is not lost if Cannes goes down the tubes.

TUESDAY, 3 MARCH, LONDON

Visit a doctor about my constipation. He asks what I'm doing about it. I tell him I am reading Joseph Goebbels's diary for 1945. He says he meant what am I eating? I tell him eight Mars Bars a day. He shakes his head and says this is what happens when you don't look after yourself properly. Then he writes a prescription for a new kind of suppository which has just come on the market. Apparently, it acts like a sort of nuclear bomb in your bowels. The results are devastating. 'Just make sure you're never more than a few feet from the nearest toilet,' says the doctor, handing me the prescription. 'This ought to do the trick. If it doesn't, I suppose we'll just have to operate.'

This evening, I call my Auntie Becky, aged 96. She lives in a nursing home near Bath. We compare bowel problems. I tell her all about the new suppository my doctor has put me on. '*Ooh*,' she says. 'I must try that.' Then she asks, 'How's your filmy thingybob coming along?'

'Oh fine,' I answer.

'I've told everybody in the nursing home all about it,' she says. 'What's it about again?'

'It's about the Cannes Film Festival, Auntie.'

'That's nice, dear,' she says. 'When's it coming on the telly?'

'Not for another year, Auntie.'

'Oh dear,' she says. 'I'll probably be dead by then.'

THURSDAY, 5 MARCH, LONDON

Success – at last! I think we may just have found our first film-maker. His name is Mike Hakata and he's just finished a movie called *Two Bad Mice*, which he's taking to Cannes. He is black and has long Rastafarian locks and a presence which turns every woman's head in the bar where we meet. Three years ago he was living in a hostel in King's Cross. He wrote *Two Bad Mice* over one weekend with the aid of a hundred fags and a bottle of whisky bought from Safeways. Then he set about raising the money to make it. The original budget was £4000. Despite never having been anywhere near a camera in his life, he managed to save enough dole money to get the thing off the ground. Also his mum lent a few quid. He found a cameraman, a sound recordist, a gaffer, a grip, a set designer and a whole bunch of actors who were prepared to work for . . . nothing. Conversations would go like this:

MIKE: I want you to be the lighting cameraman for my movie.
LIGHTING CAMERAMAN: What's your lighting budget?
MIKE: Well, to be totally honest, I was thinking we could do it without any lights at all.
LIGHTING CAMERAMAN: Without any lights.
MIKE: Yes.
LIGHTING CAMERAMAN: I'm the lighting cameraman but there aren't any lights.
MIKE: Yes. But I thought we could maybe concentrate more on the *cameraman* side of it, if you see what I mean.
LIGHTING CAMERAMAN: No. (*Beat*) How much will you pay me?
MIKE: Er – nothing.
LIGHTING CAMERAMAN: Nothing?
MIKE: Well, maybe fifty quid. It depends on Social Security.
LIGHTING CAMERAMAN: What's the budget?
MIKE Well, it's really a very low budget, if you see what I mean.
LIGHTING CAMERAMAN: No I don't. How much?

MIKE: Well, in fact, to be totally honest, sort of, well, um — nothing.

LIGHTING CAMERAMAN: Let me get this straight. You want a lighting cameraman except you've got no lights, you haven't got a budget and I don't get paid anything.

MIKE: No, no, I said maybe fifty quid.

LIGHTING CAMERAMAN: You're fucking crazy. I'll do it.

I ask Mike how he learnt about making movies. 'Well, I watch a lot of telly,' he says. 'My favourite programme is Oprah Winfrey. Also I've seen *Star Wars* fifty-six times.'

'Is *Two Bad Mice* like *Star Wars*?'

'Oh no. More like *Trainspotting* meets *The Sound of Music*.'

Mike plans to enter his movie for the Competition and Directors Fortnight — two of the most prestigious sections of the Cannes Film Festival. He's also desperate to sell it. Right now, he's broke and wearing his producer's clothes. He says he's willing to do anything to get himself and his movie noticed in Cannes.

'Like what?' I ask.

'Well, I don't know yet,' he answers. 'But I've been thinking about maybe abseiling into various offices, you know.'

'*Abseiling*?'

'Yeah, you know, maybe jump off the roof of a hotel into an office clutching a handful of trailers. I mean, the only problem is I've never abseiled before. Plus I'm terrified of heights.'

'But isn't there a danger you might . . .'

'Die. There's a danger I might die. That is a definite negative. Although it might do the movie a lot of good.'

Thus Mike Hakata. Three years ago he's in a hostel in King's Cross. Now he's taking a movie to Cannes. God knows whether he'll be successful or not. (God knows whether he'll die in the process.) I haven't seen the film yet. It might be crap. But Mike's spirit is extraordinary. He's also very funny. After two months of frustrating, desperate, back-breaking, soul-destroying research, I am convinced we have found our first story. I like Mike's energy, his crazy impulsiveness, his willingness to take risks whatever the cost. Also, his mum is very proud of him. And who am I to disappoint his mum?

FRIDAY, 6 MARCH, DUBLIN

In Dublin for the Film Festival. There are two reasons for this, namely (i) our film is partly funded by Irish tax break money which means, as well as putting a German in it, we now have to put an Irishman in it and (ii) everybody seems to think the Irish are all mad dipsomaniacs and what we need right now is a mad dipsomaniac film-maker. Hence this trip to Dublin. As everybody knows, this city is stuffed to the gills with terrific characters, all full of the blarney and having a good crack over frothy pints of the local brew before going home to tend the leprechauns in the back garden.

First stop is the Irish Film Centre, home of the Dublin Film Festival. This is run by Aine O'Halloran (pronounced 'onyer' as in 'on yer bike'). You can't get more Irish than that, I think to myself. Which is why it's a bit disconcert-ing to find she's lived in London for 40 years and speaks English like a cab driver. She is tiny and fat, and very bubbly, and I warm to her instantly. We get off to a promising start.

46

'Do you happen to know any mad dipsomaniac Irish film-makers?' I ask.

'Is the Pope Catholic?' she replies.

Aine tells me she went to Cannes for the very first time last year and discovered she was the only short fat person in the entire place. She put this down to the body police who, as everybody knows, are stationed at either end of the city during the Festival in order to stop anybody who isn't tall, thin and perfectly formed from getting in. Somehow, they must have missed her. Then she went to the Carlton Hotel, where the first person she bumped into was Francis Ford Coppola, who is extremely fat. It was soon apparent that all the short and fat people were staying at the Carlton, all of them American film producers, and all of them considerably shorter and fatter than Aine. This was a revelation and now she's looking forward to going back to Cannes in order to spend the entire festival hanging out at the Carlton feeling positively svelte among all the other fatties.

Before Dublin, Aine ran the West Belfast Film Festival. This rarely publicised cultural event – the Cannes of Ulster – takes place in a shopping mall off the Falls Road. Her biggest coup was getting the movie *Wilde* – the biopic of Oscar – to Belfast. Stephen Fry, its star, was invited to attend. After the movie, Stephen joined Aine and a group of her Irish colleagues for a drink. When it was time to go, he suddenly stood up, bowed before his audience and said: 'In the name of the British People, I would like to apologise for eight hundred years of colonial oppression. And especially that messy business with the potatoes.'

I get down to the serious business of downing several gallons of Guinness with an unending succession of Irish film-makers. It quickly becomes clear that I am paying for the drinks, with the result that most of the people I meet have absolutely nothing whatsoever to do with movies. The afternoon slowly disintegrates into a blur.

At some point I remember meeting a man with bright-orange hair and inch-thick specs, whom at first I took to be Chris Evans. Instead, he turned out to be the director of a film called *Dirty Talk*. 'It's the most sexually explicit film in the history of Irish cinema,' he said, and his glasses bobbed up and down with excitement.

Later, I met Nicholas O'Neill, a producer. 'Mine's a pint,' he said. 'Who are you?'

'My name is Stephen Walker and I'm a documentary film-maker, and I'm making a film about the Cannes Film Festival,' I answered.

'What on earth for?'

Well, I said, because, as everyone knows, Cannes is the greatest film festival in the world, the biggest showcase of movie talent, a glittering display of the brightest and best in this most magical of entertainment forms.

'No it's not,' said Nicholas. 'It's where people go to fuck.'

SUNDAY, 8 MARCH, DUBLIN

Stagger off to a lunch organised by something called the Irish Media Desk. This takes place in a restaurant near my hotel. Among the guests is a British producer I met last year. This is faintly embarrassing since she turned down my project about the aristocratic dwarfs who hunt rabbits with chihuahua dogs. The subject is not mentioned. She asks what I'm doing.

'I'm making a documentary about the Cannes Film Festival,' I tell her.

'Why would anyone want to do *that*?' she says and turns to her neighbour for the rest of the meal.

A large part of the conversation revolves around Harvey Weinstein, boss of Miramax Films and one of the last of the old-style movie tycoons. Miramax is the biggest independent film distributor in the world and Harvey is a legendary figure. Renowned for making alterations to people's movies, he's affectionately known to some in the industry as Harvey Scissorhands. (I think this is a bit unfair. Anyone who names a billion-dollar company after his mum and dad – Miriam and Max – would certainly get my mother's vote.)

The one thing that is definitely true about Harvey Weinstein is that he is extremely large which, I suppose, means he spends a lot of time at the Carlton Hotel along with all the other large people in Cannes. Apparently, he gets to see all the interesting movies two weeks before Cannes and grabs them all before anybody else has bought their plane tickets. Getting access to Harvey is a bit like winning the Lottery. I ask the others how I might persuade him to appear in my film. 'You won't,' they all answer at once. Which is a red rag to a bull if ever I saw one.

TUESDAY, 10 MARCH, NORTHERN IRELAND

Drive across the border to meet Enda Hughes, the director of *Eliminator* (the one with the longest car chase in the history of cinema). He is twenty-four and looks about eight. He shows me his prize-winning short, *Flying Saucer Rock 'n' Roll*, which is about a bunch of aliens who invade a village in South Armagh and kidnap everybody in it. It's very stylish but the acting is appalling. Enda tells me *Frock Cop* – the story of the cop who goes undercover as a transvestite and ends up rather enjoying it – won't be ready in time for Cannes. This is a bitter blow.

Before I leave, Enda shows me his pride and joy: a beautiful, 30-seat, art-deco-style cinema he and his brother built in their parents' backyard. It really is a lovely thing, complete with red swing-back seats and a swish red curtain and ancient 'Way Out' signs, and an antique 35mm projector borrowed from a local cinema which happened to have burnt down. Apparently, it was still in its projection housing pointing at the screen except, says Enda, 'The screen wasn't there.' And then, with a touch of real feeling, he adds: 'Sometimes I just sit in here and think of all the hundreds and hundreds of movies which must have clattered through that projector. It must be half a century old.'

What is it about movie buffs? They are all so unashamedly *romantic*.

Return to Dublin to watch a movie called *Pitch*, a documentary which is alarmingly similar to ours. Made by two Canadians, Kenny Holz and Spencer Rice, the film follows their hopeless attempts to pitch a screenplay at the Toronto Film Festival. The screenplay is about a Mafia hitman who goes into hospital for a routine operation on his ulcer and ends up having a sex change by mistake. As a result, he grows breasts, wears ladies' underwear and has to look for a new job (maybe a part in *Frock Cop?*).

Pitch is actually very funny, not least because Kenny and Spencer are nice Jewish boys who would happily sell their own *bubbe* to get their movie made. Also, they know absolutely nothing about the business. They crash all the parties, pitch the story to everybody (including the man who cleans the gents), waylay every agent, director, actor and distributor, thrust their script into Al Pacino's face as he walks up the red carpet and generally make a complete nuisance of themselves. As a result, they get banned from the Toronto Film Festival for ever. In addition, the film never gets made, despite a plea from Kenny Holz's mother who phones a bigshot producer and tells him how proud she is of her son and why won't he give the boy a few million dollars and make his mother happy?

Later, I meet Kenny and Spencer in a pub, and spend three hours trying to persuade them to go to Cannes this year so I won't have to do any more research on this film. They're not convinced.

I sit up half the night on the loo. I've finished with Goebbels (the Allies won) and am now on to *Barchester Towers*, by Anthony Trollope. It is 687 pages long. Trollope wrote 47 novels. This should be enough to keep me going.

FRIDAY, 13 MARCH, LONDON

Lunch with Mike Hakata at Soho House, London's glamorous media hothouse. I have the shepherd's pie. He has 20 Marlboro Lights. With him is his producer Rolf Winters, a Dutchman who picked up *Two Bad Mice* after it was shot. Rolf is very suspicious of me. He is not at all sure he wants to be involved in the film. 'I think maybe you want to make some fun of me,' he says.

'That's complete and utter and total and absolute nonsense,' I protest.

Mike tells me he's about to start work on a pop promo. A friend rang him up last week and asked if he'd do it as a favour.

'What's the budget?' asked Mike.

'Well, you see, it's not really very much,' said the friend.

'How much is not very much?'

'Well, we'd really love you to do it. As a favour, you know.'

'Yeah, but are we talking about £5000 or £500 or £50?'

'Fifty quid,' said the friend, 'is pushing it.'

And because Mike can't resist a challenge he says OK. Meanwhile, he's missed the deadline for submission to the Competition screenings. His only hope is to take *Two Bad Mice* to the Festival office in Paris and persuade them to watch it. I ask if I can come along. He agrees. He goes on the 23rd. Thus begins our first day of shooting.

I am ever more convinced that, if the premise of our story is David v. Goliath, we need a Goliath. Otherwise what's the drama? After all, the whole point of the film is to pit the little guys – like Mike Hakata – against the giants. And the biggest giant, as everybody knows, is Harvey Weinstein. If we get Harvey, we get everything: we get a story, we get tension, we get glamour, we get the richest, fattest and most powerful figure in the world of movies. And – who knows? – maybe we get an Oscar.

Fuelled by dreams of fame and glory, I've decided to devote a significant portion of my time to the chase for Harvey. What cards do I have? First off, I'm Jewish and so is he. That should count for something. Who knows, maybe we're related? The trouble with this line of argument is that *everybody* in Hollywood is Jewish and most of them probably *are* related to Harvey Weinstein. I consider maybe getting my mother to call his mother and have one of those mother-to-mother conversations, but (a) I don't have her phone number and (b) this didn't work when Kenny Holz's mother tried to do the same thing for Kenny.

The problem is, this is new territory for me. To begin with, I don't know that many film tycoons. One or two people at the BBC might just qualify, but next to Harvey they're small fry. Plus their annual budgets are what Harvey spends on his pizzas. So that's no help. What we need is something bold, something startling, something which will grab his attention and capture his interest and make him sit up and say Yes!

Then, in bed, I have a sudden brainwave: to take a whole-page ad in *Variety* with the caption:

BBC TELEVISION INVITE HARVEY WEINSTEIN TO FEATURE IN THEIR UPCOMING DOCUMENTARY ABOUT THE CANNES FILM FESTIVAL. SO YOU THINK YOU'RE TOUGH? LET'S SEE HOW TOUGH YOU REALLY ARE!

That should definitely put us on the map. On the other hand, it could ruin everything.

Should I do it?

TUESDAY, 17 MARCH, LONDON

Exactly eight weeks and one day to go before Cannes. Or 1368 hours. Or 4,924,800 seconds. The big calendar board in our office is filled with crosses, marking off the days. This morning, I noticed Hannah had turned it back to front. The reason for this is partly because she, like me, is in a state of incipient panic and partly because we are meeting a producer in the office and she does not want him to see the remarks scribbled all over the board. These are chiefly to be found under the heading CAST LIST — a joke since we don't really have a cast. The list goes like this:

GOD (E.G. HARVEY WEINSTEIN)

PENNILESS WANNABE WHO GETS REJECTED EVERYWHERE AND STAYS IN CAMP SITE (STILL TO FIND?)

SEMI-RETURED BUSINESSMAN WITH HALF-MILLION QUID TO BLOW ON ISLE OF MAN FILM (GRAHAM SIMMONDS?)

RASTAFARIAN EX-HOSTEL FILM BUFF WITH VERY VIOLENT DRUGGY MUSICAL (??) SHOT ON SOCIAL SECURITY (MIKE HAKATA)

GERMAN WITH MOVIE ABOUT BIGGEST TITS IN EUROPE (NOT GOING TO CANNES?)

GERMAN WITH MOVIE ABOUT JESUS CLONE POSS VERY, VERY BORING FOR COMIC EFFECT (HANS HORN)

Since we are now meeting large numbers of people in our office, we spend half the day shifting the board back to front and back again.

This morning's meeting is with Robert Cooper, the British producer responsible for *Truly, Madly, Deeply*. His latest movie is *Divorcing Jack*. With him is the director David Caffrey, 29, Irish and obviously very talented.

As for the meeting — it's all off the record. In fact, absolutely everything Robert Cooper says is off the record. Ask him what he had for breakfast and he'll tell you it's off the record. This is unlikely to make him a useful subject from our point of view. It's a pity since David Caffrey is a blast of fresh air. His story is not dissimilar to Mike Hakata's. Four years ago, he lived in a squat and worked on a building site.

Now he's taking a movie to Cannes, but he's still living in the squat. Things get interesting when chauffeurs turn up in limos to take him to the studio. He still can't get used to what is happening to him, nor can his mum and dad, since he managed to fail most of his exams and left school at sixteen. I suppose this gives him loads of *edge*.

WEDNESDAY, 18 MARCH, LONDON

Off to another lecture organised by the New Producers Alliance. The theme this time is 'How to Make the Perfect Pitch'. On the panel is the producer Nik Powell and Allon Reich, one of the executives behind *Trainspotting*. Alan says the difference between American producers and British producers is that American producers are very rich and British producers are very poor (although he doesn't look all that poor to me). He recalls seeing one very poor British producer at the obscenely expensive Hotel du Cap attempting to pitch an idea to an extremely rich American producer while the latter was swimming lengths in the pool. As a result, the Brit rather lost his way and ended up pitching the first half of one story and the second half of the other. The American thought it was the most brilliant idea he had ever heard and bought it there and then for five million dollars, all of which just goes to show that (a) in the movies, nobody knows anything and (b) all that exercise only makes you even more stupid than you were before.

FRIDAY, 20 MARCH, LONDON

I still don't know whether to put that ad in *Variety*. Friends in the know tell me it's bound to backfire. They say Harvey Weinstein will put pressure on every single player in Hollywood to have nothing to do with me. They say he'll chew me up and spit me out. They say if I fuck with him, on my head be it.

This morning, in a change of tactics, I write to Harvey begging him to be in our film otherwise I will set fire to myself in the lobby of Miramax.

Tessa Gogol, my American researcher, faxes me a pile of news cuttings about possible alternatives to Harvey. Two sound promising. There's Arnon Milchan, who owns a private jet and lives in an enormous pile in Malibu. And there's Joel Silver, the man who produced *Die Hard* and *Lethal Weapon*, described as 'the scariest man in Hollywood'. Silver is reputed to have said of a particular film, 'I want that movie so bad I'll stab myself in the back to get it.'

Nobody ever says that about any of my movies.

SATURDAY, 21 MARCH, LONDON

I spend part of the afternoon watching a German film called *The Three Pussies*. It consists of lots of scenes of men and women taking showers and speaking in German. Since I automatically associate Germans and showers with the Holocaust, I have some difficulties with it. It's a rotten film, anyway.

I'm smoking 30 cigarettes a day. Also my hair is going grey and wispy at the top like a baby's. Maybe I should start dyeing it. A friend of mine who does this told me it works wonders and he feels ten years younger, and nobody would ever guess. I guessed the minute his hair started to go green. The only other person I know with hair like that is my 96-year-old Auntie Becky and she looks over a hundred.

SUNDAY, 22 MARCH, LONDON

Another pile of news cuttings from Tessa in LA. She has lined up a whole host of film-makers for me to see next month. Also a few more Harvey alternatives, among them Avi Lerner, ex-Israeli paratrooper and billionaire producer of movies like *Cyborg Cop III* and *Operation Delta Force.* 'We're not trying to hide what we're doing,' he says in one article. 'If I'm making a B movie, I'm not making a C or D or Z movie. At least it comes right after A.'

Go to bed feeling sick and panicky. Eight weeks to go. Tomorrow I join Mike Hakata on the Eurostar for Paris. It will be good to get something in the can at last. Whether what I get will be good is a different matter. We will see.

At the very least, I have great hopes this movie will come right after A.

MONDAY, 23 MARCH,
WATERLOO STATION

First day of filming! This sounds more glamorous than it actually is, since I'm the only member of the crew. I'm not only directing but also asking the questions, operating the camera and recording all the sound. The official term for this is 'multi-skilling', a euphemism for having no budget. (We do have a budget – in theory – but we're still waiting on the money.) In the old days – i.e. up to two years ago – we used to employ huge crews to do the same job I'm doing now. We'd have a cameraman, a cameraman's assistant, a focus-puller, a clapper-loader, a sound recordist, a boom-swinger, at least two lighting men, a production assistant, a gaffer, a gofer, a grip, a Best Boy, a *cordon bleu* chef and an on-site masseur.

This left the director with almost nothing to do except get paid. Shifting from one location to another was like moving an entire army, a fabulously complex task which took several hours to complete and earned everyone (except the director) massive amounts of overtime. In these circumstances, 'fly-on-the-wall' film-making was something of a misnomer, since everything had to be staged at least ten times, by which point everybody was sick of the whole thing, except by then it was usually time for lunch. BBC productions laboured under a Byzantine system of penalty payments, overtime agreements and work-to-rule contracts which nobody understood, except the camera crews themselves who understood them perfectly and could recite them all backwards – and exploited them to the hilt. Whole fortunes were amassed in this way, all paid for by millions of little old ladies all over Britain who were barely able to scrape together enough for their licence fees.

To young, idealistic, enthusiastic directors like me, BBC crews were a terrifying bunch. Complete productions could be destroyed because the beer at the local pub wasn't good enough, or the spotted dick was cold or the nearest toilet was more than 20 yards away. And if you were a woman it was even worse. Being entirely fat and ugly and male, crews *hated* women. Most of all, they hated women directors. They were constitutionally incapable of understanding how a species which was put on earth to keep them in an endless supply of booze/coffee/tea/fags/Mars Bars could possibly tell them what to do. There's a well-known story of a cameraman who got so fed up with the requests of a woman director that he finally turned round to her and said, 'If you don't shut the fuck up, I'll start getting you the fucking shots you're fucking asking for.' This is what is meant when people in the BBC talk about the Good Old Days.

Now they're gone and the pendulum has swung the other way. Thanks to a combination of cheap video technology, we have to do it all ourselves. This has several distinct advantages (we don't have lots of horrible, fat ugly blokes hanging around the set doing fuck all) but it also has distinct disadvantages, chief of them being that documentaries now all look like they were shot by somebody's mother-in-law. Everything is out of focus, the sound quality is appalling, the camera shakes all over the place, the exposure is a mess, the wrong questions are asked and all the best bits of action are missed. A couple of years ago I interviewed Colin, the father of the bride, in my Jewish wedding film. I set up the camera and fixed a microphone in his jumper – something I'd never been trained to do. In the middle of the interview something funny happened to the sound. Colin's voice sounded strangely muffled through the headphones.

'Is your mike OK?' I asked.

'I think so,' he said. 'Why?'

'Your voice sounds a bit muffled.'

'It does?'

'You'd better check your mike.'

But the mike was nowhere to be found. It wasn't in his jumper. It wasn't on the floor.

Colin started fumbling with his trousers. 'I think I've found it,' he said.

'Where?' I asked.

'In my underpants.'

In fact, it was wedged in his bottom. In a way, this is a testament to the quality of modern microphones since – amazingly – I was still able to hear him. Even though he was talking out of his arse. As it were.

Mike is late. I spend half an hour standing on the concourse at Waterloo Station with a pair of headphones clamped to my ears, a couple of boxes under my arms, a microphone in my hand, a camera stuck to my spectacles and bits of wires protruding from various parts of my body. People stare at me curiously. Ten minutes before the train is due to leave, Mike arrives. With six red cans of film. And still in his producer's trousers.

He lugs the cans of film over to the barrier. 'Christ, they're fucking heavy,' he says. 'Next time, I'm definitely going to make a shorter film.'

He asks if I could help him carry the cans but I refuse, believing that, as a documentary film-maker, I should never do anything to compromise my objectivity. Also, I have a bad back.

Three hours later we arrive in Paris where I get Mike to carry his cans all over town for the camera until he threatens to pull out of my film.

TUESDAY, 24 MARCH, PARIS

This morning Mike is supposed to take his film to the offices of the Cannes Film Festival where it will be screened by judges for the Competition. The screening is fixed for twelve o'clock. By half past eleven, there's no sign of Mike. I call his room. No reply. I worry he's severely damaged his back after yesterday's efforts and am on the point of asking the concierge to unlock his door when he walks into the lobby. He looks awful. Apparently, he went to a bar last night and forgot the name of his hotel. As a result, he's spent the last eight hours wandering all over Paris. He asks me if I could lend him a pair of trousers but I tell him I couldn't possibly compromise my objectivity as a documentary film-maker and anyway we'd better get a move on because he's late.

We cross town on the Métro. Mike asks me to help with the map but I say I am not in a position to compromise my objectivity as a documentary film-maker. As a result he gets on the wrong train. We arrive at the Festival office 46 minutes late. An official wearing a very obvious hairpiece takes the six cans of film and tells Mike, in French, when he should return to collect them. Unfortunately, Mike doesn't speak French. He asks me to translate but I tell him this is not possible since he must understand it would compromise my objectivity as a documentary film-maker. As a result, Mike tells me I can fuck my documentary and hits me over the head with one of the cans of film.

We return this evening to collect the film. In execrable French, Mike asks the projectionist what he thought of it. The projectionist says according to the radio there is a distinct chance of snow. Mike thinks he's being meta-phorical, with the result that he becomes very depressed. I do my best to cheer him up by getting him to lug his six cans of film all the way across Paris back to the Gare du Nord.

On the train, I reread Tessa's notes about Joel Silver, the movie tycoon described as the scariest man in Hollywood. Apparently, he has a huge picture above his desk of a woman on the point of being beheaded. This is promising stuff. But is he going to Cannes?

Wednesday, 25 March, London

He isn't going to Cannes. Tessa's fax arrived this morning. She's still on the look-out for others. The brief is simple enough: all we need is one billionaire movie mogul with at least two private jets who bites people's heads off and is willing to do so on camera. There must be heaps of them in LA.

This afternoon my cat, Coco, was run over. In some ways this is a blessing in disguise, since Coco and I did not see eye to eye on anything. For the last three years we have been locked in a major power struggle for control over such things as who had the right to occupy the armchair nearest the TV or sleep next to my wife, Sally. Now Coco is dead and I am the victor. My daughter will be distraught. So will my wife. Coco was run over in rather a gruesome way and by the time I got to her rigor mortis had set in. To spare my daughter's feelings I popped her (Coco not my daughter) head-first into a Safeways bag but because of the rigor mortis I couldn't get the tail in as well, which meant it stuck straight up out of the bag.

When I got back, my daughter thought it was a cuddly toy. 'Is that a present for me?' she asked.

'No,' I said.

'What is it then?'

'Nothing you need worry about.'

'I know what it is,' said my daughter. 'It's a Teletubby.'

'No it isn't. Go away.'

Then my daughter started to cry. 'You don't love me any more. The only person that loves me in the whole wide world is my cat Coco.'

'Coco isn't a person,' I said.

After she went to bed, Sally and I buried Coco in the garden. This wasn't easy because the ground was very hard and I didn't have a spade. In the end, I used one of the little plastic spades my daughter has in her sandpit. By torchlight, we hacked away at the earth and finally managed to stick Coco in, tail and all, still in the Safeways bag. Several times I caught sight of one or two neighbours watching me curiously from their upstairs windows. They'll be checking the drains next.

Thursday, 26 March, London

This morning Coco's son, Jaffa, went out into the garden. After a few moments he started pawing at the grave.

'Oh look,' said Sally. 'He's found his mummy. Oh dear, that's so terribly sad. Cats are really just like humans, you know.' Just as she said this, Jaffa lifted up his leg and peed all over his mother's grave.

This afternoon, I meet Aaron Simpson and Frank Mannion, two twenty-something hotshot producers straight out of *The Player*. Frank is tall, thin, bespectacled and Irish. Aaron is small and fat. I like them immediately.

Aaron says, 'We are the best fucking producers in the business.'

Talking to Aaron and Frank is a bit difficult because their mobile phones (they have one each) keep going off the whole time. But they're very entertaining. They're also very direct. I say, 'Tell me what you think of X' (X being a famous actor/director/producer/tycoon).

'We can't possibly,' says Frank.

'We really couldn't,' says Aaron.

But they tell me anyway. They just can't help themselves.

Afterwards Frank says, 'Our only concern is that, if we did your film, we don't want to come out of it looking like complete twats,' to which I say, 'You couldn't be further from the truth.' Which is, of course, the truth.

We stick their names up on the board.

This evening I put my daughter to bed. She says, 'Have you been playing in my sandpit, Daddy?'

'What?'

'Have you been in my sandpit?'

'Of course not. Don't be silly. Go to sleep.'

'My spade's gone all funny in the middle and Mummy said to ask Daddy.'

'I don't know what you're talking about. Did Mummy say that?'

'Yes, she did. But Daddy?'

'What?'

'My friend Sophie at school says cats don't go to heaven or hell, they go to limbo. What's limbo?'

'It's a very nice place with lots of trees for cats to climb and mice for them to catch.'

But what I really mean is, it's where I am right now.

SUNDAY 29 MARCH, LONDON

Last night I dreamt I went to Cannes for the Film Festival but nobody was there. The streets are deserted. The hotels, bars, restaurants and cinemas are all empty. Even my own crew haven't turned up. I have my camera with me but there is nothing to film. I wander the streets in a desperate search for one film-maker, *any* film-maker, to film. But there is only me. I wake up, uncertain whether this is a nightmare of egomaniacal proportions or a terrible foretaste of the future.

Whatever the case, I have a horrible feeling that the final joke is going to be on me.

MONDAY, 30 MARCH, LONDON

Meet Mike in Soho, carrying his six cans of film. He's still wearing his producer's clothes. By now, these look like they've been dug up from somebody's grave. He's also smoking a hundred roll-ups a day. To date, he hasn't heard whether his film has got into Competition or not. Now he's taking his movie to Mr Young's Cinema where it's to be screened by Pierre-Henri Deleau, the head of Directors Fortnight. This is the next most prestigious section of the Festival after the Competition. I film Mike carrying his cans to the cinema. He tells me about a dream he had last night in which out of a thousand submissions his movie was chosen for the Competition. We compare dreams and agree that I came off worse.

What Mike doesn't know is that we've been given permission to film the actual screening in Mr Young's. Nobody has ever managed to film these screenings. They are strictly private events. Last week, my producer Pascale and Pierre-Henri Deleau had dinner together in Paris and he made lots of flattering remarks about her. I don't know whether that had anything to do with it, but anyway she's secured unprecedented access to film the screening. She should get a medal. (She should also have dinner with Harvey Weinstein.)

Pierre-Henri turns up looking very dapper in a camel-hair coat, beautifully pressed trousers and shoes you can see your own reflection in. He kisses Pascale on both cheeks and asks her to dinner. I am not invited.

Pierre-Henri spends a strange sort of life sitting in darkened cinemas all over the world watching movies. Today he hopes to get through six or seven of them and his schedule is tight. We start with Mike's. I watch Mr Young, the projectionist, as he opens the first of Mike's six cans of film and threads it through the projector. At last I shall see what it's like. Will I love it? Will I hate it? Then the lights dim, the projector starts up, the film turns through the gate and there, up on the screen in front of me, is . . . Mike's movie.

Well. I *quite* like it. Mike once told me he spent most of his dole money going to art house movies. This is the result. The film is a strange hybrid of bits of other people's work, a dash of Godard here, a dollop of Kurosawa there, a smattering of Fellini in this scene, of Renoir in that (there's no sign of Oprah Winfrey though – or *Star Wars*). It's not a *bad* film – in fact, it's amazingly beautiful in parts – and it's got a few funny bits and a few sad bits and a few romantic bits – and it's got a terrific soundtrack – and don't forget it's his first movie – and it was made for about ten quid – but . . . the truth is, it doesn't touch me. The story is ostensibly about a black man and a white man who are in fact the same person, and there's a murder in it and a rather stylish love-making scene and a very sinister drug pusher and there's a priest who's also not a priest and somebody gets hit over the head with a saucepan and . . . and so it goes on. Except it doesn't because Pierre-Henri Deleau stops the film after the second reel.

'He's never done that before,' says Mr Young. 'He must really *hate* it.'

'Did you hate it?' I ask Pierre-Henri.

'Yes,' he replies.

'Oh dear,' I say

He consults his notes. 'Hakata. 'Ha-ka-ta. He is Japanese, I think.'

66

On the way out, Mr Young says, 'Oh, well, that's another one down the drain.'

When I get home, Mike calls. 'Do you know,' he says, 'I don't know why but I have this funny feeling they just *loved* the movie.'

WEDNESDAY, 1 APRIL, LONDON

A meeting with my bank manager. We are, it appears, completely broke. For the past six weeks I haven't dared to open my bank statements. My bank manager says I have an overdraft of £11,564 and asks me how I intend to clear it. I am at a loss to enlighten him. I try to win his sympathy by telling him all about how Coco was run over but he isn't buying it. I leave, promising not to write another cheque, and promptly go to Hammersmith Shopping Centre and write six cheques totalling £365. In WH Smith, I buy Richard E. Grant's diary in which Richard E. Grant describes going every day to WH Smith instead of getting himself a proper job.

I do have a proper job – of sorts – but the problem is I haven't been paid for two months. This afternoon, I ring up my agent.

CUT TO:

INT. MY OFFICE. DAY.

FX Dialling tone. A voice answers. This is my agent.

67

MY AGENT

What's up?

ME

I have an overdraft of £11,564.

MY AGENT

That must be awful. (*Beat*) So what are you going to do about it?

ME

Well, I sort of thought that was your job.

MY AGENT

Don't be silly. I'm off to Istanbul tomorrow.

ME

Oh. When do you get back?

MY AGENT

Thursday. But it's no good calling me then. I'm away in Sri Lanka for two weeks. Tell you what. I'll call you when I return.

ME

Oh. Right.

MY AGENT

God, I need a holiday.*

THURSDAY, 2 APRIL, LONDON

One of the reasons I always wanted to work in the movies was to be surrounded by beautiful actresses. It hasn't quite

* Actually she got me my money in the end. And she's a terrific agent.

worked out that way. Everybody thinks that in the movies the casting couch is king, but it's not my experience. Of course, you hear things all the time. For instance, I heard recently about one famous producer who was notorious for casting on the couch. In fact, he used to film actresses taking all their clothes off. Sometimes he got so excited he forgot to take the lens cap off. In the BBC, nobody does anything like that (although I've often forgotten to take the lens cap off). The closest, I suppose, is a notorious executive in the Eighties who regularly chastised innocent young secretaries until he was finally chucked out. He was affectionately known as Number 33, since if you pressed that number on the BBC coffee machine you got it 'white & whipped'. I believe he's emigrated to America now.

I once thought I was going to be cast on the couch by my ex-boss. She was (and still is) a very sexy woman and she frequently wore a crisp black blouse which made her look like the sort of naughty headmistress often to be found in dirty adolescent minds (like mine). On one occasion, I remember, she called me into her office ostensibly to discuss the script I was working on. It was quite late and everybody else had gone home. She was wearing her crisp black blouse. I went in and she immediately shut the door. Then she locked it. Then she turned to me and said, 'Now we won't be disturbed.' I could barely contain my excitement. I couldn't keep my eyes off that crisp black blouse. What secrets lay beneath it? I wondered. What wonders, what joys, what pleasures, what mysteries? Then she turned to me and said, 'Where's the script? I'm not at all sure about page two.'

And that was that.

Friday, 3 April, London

Still no word from Harvey. He must have got my letter by
now. I think it's a but rude of him, especially since I said I'd
set fire to myself in the lobby of Miramax if he didn't agree
to be in my film. If somebody said that to me, the least I'd
do is reply.

I've been looking at lots of pictures of Harvey so that if
I do have to go to Miramax I'll know what he looks like.
What he looks like is an extra in a James Cagney gangster
movie. He's the guy who always gets shot in the second reel.

Lunch at the Groucho Club with Graham Simmonds, the
Isle of Man businessman turned producer with half a
million quid of his wife's pension money to spend on
movies. His wife, apparently, thinks this is just 'one of
Graham's little wheezes', which is awfully generous of her,
considering. (Actually, that bit about the pension isn't true —
it's actually all his own money.)

Graham turns out to be awfully nice and awfully naïve.
He still talks like the Queen, albeit with a northern accent.
Things don't seem to have moved far with his Isle of Man
project. He's still keen to do lots of filming on the Isle of
Man itself, but since the millionaire businessman in the story
has mutated into a Texan from Dallas he now needs to find
somewhere that looks like Dallas. After several weeks'
research he's discovered that nowhere on the Isle of Man
looks anything like Dallas. So now it's Liverpool.

'Why Liverpool?' I ask.

'Well, you see, there are bits of Liverpool which look
exactly like Dallas,' says Graham. 'Not many people know
that.'

I ask if he's got a script yet.

'No,' he admits. 'But we do not think the absence of a script will necessarily create difficulties of an especially insuperable nature.'

'Sorry?'

'There's not much dialogue in it, you see. We regard this as more – music-led.'

'What sort of music?'

'Seventies music,' Graham tells me. 'You know – like *The Graduate.*'

'That was the Sixties.'

'Was it?' says Graham. 'I don't go to that many movies.'

On reflection, I'm not sure Graham is such a good idea for us. He's a bit vulnerable and I'm very fond of him. I remember what happened to Bernie Adelberry, the caterer in my Jewish wedding film. Bernie was twenty-five stone and adored his job more than anything else in the world. 'If there's one thing I love,' he used to say, 'it's a really good nosh.' He was so fat he could barely walk. In the film you saw him preparing for a wedding in the kitchens. He tasted everything. At one point he stuck his spoon into a huge vat of chocolate sauce. 'Mmm,' said Bernie, licking the spoon, 'now *that* is what I call delicious. In fact, it's so delicious I think I might just have another little taste.' Then he put the (same) spoon back into the chocolate sauce and licked it all off again. As a result, all the Jewish mothers in Great Britain probably fainted with horror. My mum certainly did. She also swore she'd never hire Bernie Adelberry for any of *her* daughters' weddings.

As for me, I felt terribly guilty. The last thing I wanted to do was hurt the man. And now I feel the same about Graham. It's too easy. I'm too responsible. Forget it. Leave the man alone. And the best of luck to him.

SATURDAY, 4 APRIL, LONDON

A terrible night. This morning, I study myself in the mirror with horror. What I see is not me but my father. I am definitely growing breasts. My stomach sticks out in such a way that it is a distinct shock to find I still own a penis. My face is getting all jowly and I have lines on my forehead like Clapham Junction. People say I look permanently worried. I tell them this is because I *am* permanently worried. I am approaching 36 and clearly On the Way Down. This film isn't helping.

What's left of the day is spent closeted in the office with Pascale and Brian Raftery. Brian is our production manager, which means he supervises the budget and makes sure I don't spend more than I've got. Since (so I'm told) I have an appalling reputation for spending far more than I've got, I expect Brian to be a tough old bastard who says no to everything. The opposite is the case. He's awfully nice and says yes to everything. We get on famously. Either he's a brilliant actor or he's mad enough to believe I know what I'm doing.

There are six weeks to go before Cannes. Thanks to Brian, everything is ready. Our cameramen, our sound recordists, our production assistants, our equipment, our lights, our apartments, our office, our fax machines, our mobile phones, our film stock, our dinner suits – everything is booked. Everything is sorted. There's no turning back. We're hooked in, fixed up, strapped down, ready to go. The only thing still missing is . . . *a story.*

OK. What have we got? We've got Mike Hakata. Who knows what's going to happen to him? His film isn't a masterpiece, although on reflection this may be to our advantage. He'll have to work that much harder to sell it.

He'll have to do some crazy stunts (like abseil into offices) and take some major risks (like . . . *get killed*). That's a definite plus. On the debit side . . . nothing may happen. He may not sell the movie. Moreover, if he hasn't changed his trousers by the time we're in Cannes I'm not going anywhere near him. We'll have to shoot the whole thing with a telescopic lens.

But at least Mike exists. Right now, he's all we've got. There's nobody else. No Harvey Weinstein, no German, no Irishman, nothing. One by one the names are being wiped off the board. This one's too boring, that one's not going to Cannes, this one doesn't know if he wants to be in the film, that one knows he doesn't. Of course, I've still got my trip to the States next week. There *must* be somebody out there. And I may go to Germany again. And something may turn up. And miracles do happen. And six weeks is six weeks. And I say my prayers every night. And I always give generously to charity. Meanwhile, Cannes isn't waiting for us.

Faced with impending catastrophe, I decide the best thing to do is pretend it isn't happening. When Brian says, 'How's it going then?' I say, 'Terrific.' He says, 'Good characters?' and I say, 'Fantastic.' He says, 'Interesting stories?' I say, 'Amazing.' He says, 'Funny?' I say, 'Funny? *Funny?* They'll be rolling in the aisles.' And so it goes on until I start to believe it myself.

Joseph Goebbels did the same thing in 1945. Until he committed suicide.

MONDAY, 6 APRIL, LONDON

Wake up from a dream in which Harvey Weinstein personally goes down on his knees and absolutely begs me to include him in our film, otherwise he will set fire to himself in my office. These days, this is the closest I ever get to a wet dream.

After lunch, I meet Dennis Davidson. Dennis Davidson runs the most powerful PR company in the universe. The company is called Dennis Davidson Associates. Apparently, nothing moves in Cannes without Dennis Davidson or one of his Associates behind it. He runs the whole show. He runs the parties, he books the cinemas, he organises the stars, he sorts out where they sleep, when they sleep, whom they talk to, how long they talk to them, what they talk about and when they go to the loo. (He probably books all the loos as well.) Any suspicion I might have that Cannes is actually a genuinely spontaneous event is instantly extinguished after meeting Dennis. In fact, the whole thing is clearly a PR event from first to last, a sort of Disneyland in which everything is manufactured, manipulated and sterile. One must live in the real world, however, and in the real world I need Dennis Davidson much more than he needs me. I sit in his office and smile a great deal, and ask for his help.

Like all supremely powerful people, he says it's not in his power. 'I'm just one of the little guys,' he explains. At this point his secretary puts her head round the door, and says that X (a Very Important Producer?) is on the phone. 'Tell him I'm busy,' snaps Dennis.

Tomorrow I join Pascale and Brian in Cannes. This, of course, is a useful opportunity to scout locations, meet lots of key people and generally do a great deal of very hard work. The one thing it's definitely not is a holiday.

TUESDAY, 7 APRIL, CANNES

Well, here I am in a pretty restaurant on the Croisette guzzling *moules frites* in the sunshine and writing postcards to all my friends back home. Life could be worse. (I could be making a film about the Cannes Film Festival, for example.) The Croisette, by the way, is the famous palm-fringed promenade which stretches from one end of the town to the other. Today it's relatively empty but everybody tells me that during the Festival it is stuffed to the brim with movie people. All the locals get the hell out and rent their apartments at exorbitant prices. Right in front of me is the famous marina, where everybody parks their yachts. This isn't empty, since the Television Festival – a sort of poor relation to the Film Festival – opens tomorrow.

Years ago, I came here for the TV Festival. I'd made a film about a bunch of Vietnam veterans returning to Vietnam which was co-produced by a French channel. They brought the film here, to present it. On the second day I was invited aboard the BBC yacht. I never knew the BBC *had* a yacht. In fact, I thought the BBC was desperately hard up for cash. That's what they were telling the licence fee payers at any rate. Budgets were being slashed, staff were being fired, resources were being cut. On the very day I arrived in Cannes, the BBC unions called a massive strike. Thousands of people downed tools, and picket lines were set up outside all the major production centres across the country. And now it turned out they had this *yacht*. And not just any old yacht, either. It was a great big yacht, the biggest in the harbour. And it was full of gorgeous, lithe, suntanned women (were they all there buying TV programmes?) and gallons of champagne, and charming waiters and lots of nice things to eat off little silver trays. There was only one thing missing and that was . . . the name of the boat. It didn't seem to have a name. It wasn't on the invitation. A sheet had been crudely draped where it should have been, over the side. If you looked closely, you could just make out the letter H. H for what? I'll tell you what. H for . . . *Hedonist B.*

No wonder they had to raise the licence fee.

Today there's no sign of the *Hedonist B.* We spend half an hour in the marina and then move on to the Palais des Festivals. This is the heart of the Film Festival. Principally, it's where the Competition screenings are held, the location for those famous steps with the red carpets and the stars and the paparazzi and the frenzied crowds of fans – all the things which give Cannes its sheen of glamour.

The reality is very different. The old Palais was demolished a few years ago and replaced with a hideous hunk of building, which looks like a cross between a provincial shopping mall and a nuclear bomb shelter. Everyone calls it the Bunker. It isn't just a home to the Film Festival. In fact, it's a sort of Cannes version of Olympia. Each week it houses a different event. For instance, in October there's the World Tax-Free Convention where duty-free salesmen come from all over the world and turn the Palais into a giant version of Dubai airport. And immediately after the Film Festival there's the International Dentists Convention. I'm told it's not unknown for film-makers to get their dates slightly wrong with the result that they end up trying to sell their movie to a bunch of dentists.

The thing about the Bunker is it's very deep. It goes down several floors. During the Film Festival, each floor is given up to hundreds of stalls advertising and selling movies. People spend fifteen hours a day down there never seeing daylight. Like a sort of Dante's vision of hell, the deeper you go, the worse the product. By the time you get to the bottom, it's all horror movies and porn videos. Apparently, the porn people have a yacht too and it's even bigger than the *Hedonist B.* (It's the *Hedonist A.*) I'm told they throw the most outrageous party in Cannes, in effect a sort of giant orgy on the yacht. Everybody tries to get an invitation and almost everybody fails. We, of course, will make every effort to include it in our documentary.

Pascale has done a great job securing access to the Bunker. Sadly, she hasn't managed to do the same for the Hotel du Cap, the fabulously expensive hostelry up in the hills outside Cannes where only the very richest and the most famous stay during the Festival (Harvey Weinstein stays there). The average cost of a bedroom the size of a shoebox is $3000 a night and they only accept cash. This is withdrawn from the vaults of major banks and delivered personally to the hotel manager either in wheelbarrows or large trucks, depending on the size of the bedroom. It's one of the great Cannes traditions.

The other thing about the Hotel du Cap is that they hate all journalists. They *loathe* them. This is why we can't film there. Brian says we might be able to film illicitly in the hotel since he's discovered a camera which fits into your tie and is so small it can't be seen. This sounds like an excellent idea, although there's always the danger the wearer of the tie might get spotted and end up in jail. I tell Brian I think he should wear it. I don't like ties anyway.

This evening, we crash the *Canal Plus* party where a woman hands me a little plastic bag with a pill in it. On the bag is a label which says: CONFIDENCE PILL FOR DIRECTORS.

How did she know?

Thursday, 9 April, London

D-Day for Mike Hakata. This morning he learns what I already know: that his movie has been rejected by both the Competition and Directors Fortnight. I'm there to film the moment. When I arrive, Mike says, 'God I want this more than anything else in the world.' I've never seen him so nervous.

His producer Rolf says, 'Everything is going to be fine. I've got a bottle of champagne in the fridge.'

When the phone rings they both jump. Rolf takes the call. It's from Christian Jeune, one of the Competition officials. He tells Rolf *Two Bad Mice* has not been selected. Five minutes later the phone rings again. This time it's a woman from Directors Fortnight. She says she's sorry, but the film hasn't been selected. Mike looks close to tears. For a few moments he's unable to speak.

Rolf puts a consoling arm round his shoulder. 'Fuck 'em,' he says. 'It's a great movie.'

Is it great? I don't know. What is great is that Mike ever made it in the first place, against such overwhelming odds. But they don't give prizes for that.

'Don't let me down now,' says Rolf. 'We'll show the bastards.'

'I suppose so,' says Mike. But they don't open the bottle of champagne.

The awful thing about all this is that we knew and they didn't. We knew they'd been rejected, but could not say so. We knew Pierre-Henri Deleau had stopped the film in the second reel because he hated it — but they didn't. As far as Mike is concerned I haven't even seen the film yet. He says, 'I really hope you like it.'

And I say, 'I'm sure I will.'

*

Later, in the office, we watch the tape I've shot. Pascale says, 'That's terribly moving.'

Hannah says, 'Poor bastard.'

Bronwen says, 'There won't be a dry eye in the house.'

As for me, I don't say anything.

FRIDAY, 10 APRIL, LONDON

This morning I suddenly remember I've got six rolls of unexposed 16mm stock sitting in my attic. Six rolls is 60 minutes' worth. It's mostly leftover bits and pieces from my old films. Some of it is time-expired, but it's probably still OK. I ring Mike and tell him he can have the lot for his next movie on condition that he lets me interview his mum. (I've been trying to interview her for weeks but he keeps saying no.) He agrees instantly, which only goes to show he is the sort of director who will sell his own mother for a movie.

Tomorrow I go to the States. The afternoon is spent packing. Tessa faxes a whole pile of news cuttings for me to read on the plane. One of them is about a guy called Mike De Luca, the thirty-one-year-old president of production at New Line Pictures. Five years ago nobody had ever heard of him. Now he's a millionaire, he's Iron Mike, he's King of the Heap, he's the next Harvey Weinstein. Everybody beats a path to his door. Also he chucks money around like confetti: $65 million for *The Long Kiss Goodnight*, $16.5 million for Bruce Willis in *Last Man Standing*, $2.5 million for a four-page treatment by Joe Eszterhas called *One Night Stand*. (*One Night Stand* was a sleazy sex thriller in which gorgeous women had sex with gorgeous men saying, 'God it feels like the Niagara Falls down there.' It was a total flop.) For four pages, $2.5m is pretty impressive by any standards (by my reckoning this paragraph would be worth $600,000) and I ask Tessa to try and set up a meeting. Who knows, I might even write a couple of pages for the guy.

This evening, I ring up my 96-year-old Auntie Becky.

'I'm going to Los Angeles tomorrow, Auntie,' I say.

'That's nice, dear,' my Auntie Becky says. 'Are you driving?'

'No, it's in America. You know, where they make the pictures.'

'I don't go to the pictures much nowadays,' says my Auntie Becky. 'Not with my legs. They showed us a picture here the other day. It was called *Four Thingies and a Thingie*. Cary Grant was in it.'

'Isn't it Hugh Grant?'

'It was all swear-words anyway,' says my Auntie Becky.

SATURDAY, 11 APRIL, 37,000 FEET
EN ROUTE FOR LA

The airline stewardess says this is a non-smoking flight. In addition, she says there are smoke detectors in the toilets and that anyone caught tampering with them will be subject to a fine of $5000, after which they will be stripped naked, strung up from the overhead luggage compartments and disembowelled in front of all the other passengers as a warning. The flight lasts for exactly ten hours and forty-one minutes. I spend the entire time furiously chewing gum.

SUNDAY, 12 APRIL, LOS ANGELES

Wake up to the sun rising over the Pacific. I am in a non-smoking room. The desk clerk informs me that anyone caught smoking will be subject to a fine of one million dollars, after which they will be stripped naked, disembowelled and strung up in the lobby in front of all the other guests as a warning. Persistent offenders will also have their testicles removed with a blunt knife. I ask the clerk where I can buy more chewing gum since I've run out.

So here I am again: Los Angeles, California – a billion cars, a billion freeways, a billion horrible movies. And the movies are the worst of it. After two days here your brain rots with sheer boredom. Nobody talks about anything else. Everybody's in development, everybody's in production, everybody's got a script, everybody is pitching, selling, buying, dealing, fighting, begging movies 24 hours a day, 365 days a year. It's a terrible way to spend a life.

Last time I was here was three years ago, when I was casting my drama *Prisoners In Time*. I needed a Japanese actor who could speak English and since I couldn't find one in Japan I came to LA. Japanese-American actors are thick on the ground here. They're almost always out of work. Occasionally, they get to play bit parts as Korean drug dealers or Chinese Triad killers. They hardly ever get to play themselves. I met them all, including my hero, the guy who says 'Warp factor 5, Captain' in *Star Trek*. (He didn't get the part, but we had an interesting discussion about Vulcan sexual deviancy.) The whole thing was a bit traumatic for me since I'd never worked with actors before, but I took some comfort from the fact that the great Louis Malle had the same problem when he did his first drama in 1959. His only previous movie was an underwater documentary with Jacques Cousteau, which meant that all he'd ever directed were fish. But he went on to a glittering future. I suppose, from a director's point of view, there's not much difference between an actor and a Dover sole.

Monday, 13 April, Los Angeles

I meet Tessa in a non-smoking coffee shop (fine $3m). She looks radiant. She came out here from England with her husband – an art director – four years ago. Today, he works for Steven Spielberg. Since then, they've never looked back.

Together we drive over to Venice Beach to meet the first in a long list of directors she's lined up for me. Ann Boehlke is a director who is married to her producer, Mac Polhemus. I spend most of the first hour working out how to pronounce their names. Ann and Mac have mortgaged everything they own to make their first feature, *A Scottish Tale*. This was shot exclusively in Northern California. Since Northern California looks nothing like Scotland, Ann and Mac decided to add lots of bagpipe music to the soundtrack. As a result, it looks like a film set in Northern California – with bagpipe music.

Ann shows me a massive file full of rejection letters from hundreds of film festivals all over America. Then she shows me another full of rejection letters from distributors; then another full of rejection letters from sales agents. She has wardrobes full of rejection letters. Each one is carefully filed away, tabulated, recorded, preserved. She and her husband are living on nothing. They have an 18-month-old daughter to feed. They can't afford to pay the rent. They can't face their friends any more since every friend they have put money into the movie. One of their only successes was a prize for Best Student Feature from something called the Hardcore Film Festival. The Hardcore Film Festival is a DIY operation run by a bloke who shows movies to a bunch of neighbours in his backyard. The award itself is a broken Super 8mm plastic reel mounted on a piece of cardboard. It sits next to the kitchen sink. Meanwhile, Ann and Mac have almost nothing to eat.

Why do they do it?

I spend another half-hour in their tiny flat, with their little toddler wandering about, with the fat files of rejection letters piled on the kitchen table, with the plastic award sitting next to the sink, and the whole, awful, soul-destroying, hope-denying, dream-shattering reality of independent film-making hits me like a kick in the balls.

Oh, and I almost forgot. Ann is going to Cannes to try to sell the film. But Mac isn't. He's staying behind to look after their daughter. As he tells me just before I leave, he's had enough.

TUESDAY, 14 APRIL, LOS ANGELES

Still no word from Harvey Weinstein. Doesn't he know I'm in town?

Meanwhile, I have appointments with three other tycoons. Number one is Avi Lerner, the multimillionaire ex-Israeli paratrooper turned movie mogul. He runs a company called Nu Image, churning out hundreds of lookalike low-budget B movie flicks with titles like *Warhead, Search and Destroy* and *No Code of Conduct*. None of them ever wins an Oscar but they all make money — lots of it. Part of the reason Lerner makes so much money is because he doesn't spend it. Budgets are pared down to the minimum. Movies like *Titanic* leave him cold. He says, 'If I gave my son two hundred million to play around with, he could make the same picture.' If *my* father gave me two hundred million to play around with, I'd get out of this business.

Nu Image's offices are on Sunset Boulevard. The exterior is dominated by a massive brass door 60 feet high, several feet thick, studded with hieroglyphics. The whole thing looks like a cross between an Egyptian tomb and an air raid shelter. It's not clear whether this is an exercise in vanity or a sensible precaution against the threat of attack. After all, the guy used to be an Israeli paratrooper. Now he produces movies. Maybe he's also worried about the various animal rights groups who've been after his blood ever since a flock of birds were blown to smithereens by mistake in *No Code of Conduct*.

A secretary leads me to Lerner's office. The corridors are splattered with posters of his movies. But for the titles, they all look exactly the same: the same guns, missiles, tanks, bombs and explosions. (According to one of Lerner's associates, he's the kind of guy who feels safe around explosions.) I remember reading how one of his productions was running into difficulties with its star, Mickey Rourke. Mickey was having a tantrum and had holed himself up in his trailer. Nobody could get him out. As a result, the production had ground to a halt, the crew were doing nothing, millions of dollars were being wasted. Everybody begged, entreated, pleaded with Mickey to come out of his trailer – without success. Then they called Lerner. He flew out to the location, went up to Mickey's trailer, knocked on the door. He told Mickey he had friends in Mossad, the Israeli secret service, and if he didn't come out, they would blow up the trailer. Mickey came out.

It's therefore a shock to find that Avi Lerner – if

appearances are anything to go by — is a complete softie. Most of our meeting he spends on the phone to his wife in London. He says, 'Yes, dear, I promise I'll look after that cold' and 'No, dear, I won't stay up late tonight' and 'Of course, dear, I'll go see the doctor tomorrow.' I am instantly disheartened. Is this the guy who threatened to blow up Mickey Rourke in his trailer? Is this the guy who feels safe around explosions? Is this the guy the American Humane Society have put on their hit list?

Forget it. He's too nice. Right now, we don't need nice. We need nasty. And anyway, he isn't even sure he's going to Cannes. I strike him off the list.

My appointment with Mogul Number Two is after lunch. For legal reasons, I can't give his real name. Let's just say he's even bigger than Avi Lerner. A major-league player. Amazingly, Tessa managed to get an interview with him, despite the fact that he loathes publicity and is known to sue at the drop of a hat (hence the anonymity). Like all the Big Players round here, he inhabits a vast suite of offices in the middle of the studio lot. Batteries of secretaries guard his door. The office itself has no windows. Mogul Number Two sits behind a desk significantly wider than my normal field of vision. There is absolutely nothing on it except a telephone.

CUT TO:

INT. MOGUL NUMBER TWO'S OFFICE. DAY.

A tough, wiry, no-nonsense sort of guy sits behind his desk smoking a cigar. Just as I enter, he slams down the phone.

MOGUL NUMBER TWO

Fucking stars! They all want the fucking earth? Why should I give them the fucking earth! Am I God? Am I Moses? Am I the President of the United States? Where do you want me to sit?

ME
(*confused*)
I'm sorry?

MOGUL NUMBER TWO

To sit. Where do you want me? You got enough light in here? We can go to the boardroom if you like. Is my hair OK? Maybe my nose needs some powder. You think I need some powder on my nose?

ME

Er – I think there's been a mis . . .

MOGUL NUMBER TWO

What about my suit? You like my suit? My wife bought it for me. Her family were in *shmutter*. That's how she knows from a good suit. If you don't like it I can change it. You sure I don't need some powder on my nose? Maybe just a little?

ME

But, you see, I'm not actually here to . . .

MOGUL NUMBER TWO

We only got twenty minutes. I'd make it longer but I got some *shlemiel* from the BBC coming to see me. He's doing a movie about Cannes. I ask you, what does he want to talk to me for? I hate the fucking place. Are you sure my nose is OK?

So much for Mogul Number Two. I strike *him* off the list too.

Mogul Number Three is Mike Medavoy, former boss of

86

Columbia, now boss of Phoenix Pictures. This time I call in advance. I don't want any more misunderstandings. A perfectly groomed assistant leads me into a waiting room. 'Mike is on the phone right now,' he says. 'He'll be with you shortly.'

He isn't with me shortly. He isn't with me for three-quarters of an hour. I sit in the room and look at the walls, every square inch of which is filled with hundreds of photographs of . . . Mike Medavoy. There's Mike with Francis Coppola, Mike with Dennis Hopper, Mike with Michelle Pfeiffer, Mike with Winston Churchill, Mike with Abraham Lincoln, Mike receiving the Ten Commandments on Mount Sinai. Everybody who is anybody, Mike knows them. Everywhere I look there's Mike, grinning for the camera.

Then another perfectly groomed assistant enters the room. 'Mike can give you seventeen minutes,' he says. 'He's a very busy man. Follow me.' He ushers me into what I suppose is Mike's office. I sit down. The assistant recoils in horror. '*Not there!* That's Mike's special chair. *Nobody* ever sits there. You sit . . . here.' He points to a much more uncomfortable-looking chair. 'Remember,' he adds, 'you've only got seventeen minutes.'

The room looks like it's been designed by Albert Speer. It's absolutely vast. More photos of Mike glare from the walls. Statues (of Mike?) fill the corners. Never-to-be-read books sit, perfectly aligned, on coffee tables. Then Mike enters the room. Of course I recognise him immediately. He's the guy in all the photos.

'We've only got seventeen minutes,' he says. 'I have a very busy schedule.' He sits down on his special chair. 'I'm sorry — what was your name again?' He wears a crisp, starched shirt, a perfectly pressed tie, immaculately polished shoes. The creases in his trousers are razor-sharp. He looks like the kind of man who washes his hands a lot. The conversation turns, in a desultory way, to Cannes. For sixteen of my seventeen minutes, Medavoy tells me all about the Special Lifetime Achievement Award they're giving him for being one of the all-time greatest film producers in the world. 'Of course,' he says, 'I'm very flattered. It's awfully nice of them. I shall be staying at the Hotel du Cap.' He brushes an invisible speck of dust from his trousers. 'I suppose you'll probably want to film me,' he says. Then he looks at his watch. 'I'm afraid our time is up. It's been – a pleasure meeting you. What was your name again?'

Sixty seconds later I am out on the street, permanently erased from Mike Medavoy's memory.

Go back to my hotel to find a fax from the office. Apparently, Miramax have called about Harvey. The call was very polite but basically boiled down to two words: Fuck Off.

So that's it, then. No Harvey. No Miramax. No Mogul. Where does that leave me? It leaves me – nowhere. I've got no replacement. Avi Lerner doesn't know who the hell I am. And Mike Medavoy – well, forget Mike Medavoy (he's already forgotten me). Plus I haven't got an American director yet. I haven't got anything yet. I lie on my bed feeling sick, depressed and beaten. I've only got one more month. Why don't I just admit defeat? Why don't I chuck the whole thing in? It's obvious this movie is going to be *terrible*.

THURSDAY, 16 APRIL, LOS ANGELES

In brilliant sunshine, Tessa and I drive over to Hermosa beach. In a non-smoking coffee shop (fine $8 billion) I meet

Jason McCue, a young producer who has made two movies, *Cannibal the Musical* and *Orgazmo*. The first he describes as *Friday the Thirteenth* meets *My Fair Lady*. The second is about a young virginal Mormon who becomes a major porn star. The actor who plays the Mormon sits with us in the coffee shop. He is about four feet tall with terrible acne and watery eyes. Throughout the entire conversation, he fixes me with a fish-eye gaze.

Jason is taking *Cannibal the Musical* to Cannes with loads of T-shirts he hopes to sell in order to finance his next movie. The T-shirts are marketed through his company CRAP – short for Certified Renegade American Product. Since his next movie features a major star, he needs to sell several million T-shirts. While in Cannes, he's also intending to set up a rival film festival, called Cannes You Dig It? The festival will feature only one film (*Cannibal the Musical*). It will offer a number of prizes (Best Film, Best Director, Best Actor, Best T-Shirt) all of which are expected to be won by *Cannibal the Musical*. Everybody who attends the prize giving will be obliged to buy a thousand T-shirts each. No French will be admitted. The whole enterprise, Jason tells me, is designed (a) to make Jason McCue famous all over Cannes and (b) to piss off the French.

Jason also tells me he is currently 'in discussion' with Lloyd Kaufman, the famous B movie producer and boss of Troma Films (whom I shall be meeting in New York next week). Jason says Lloyd Kaufman has two passions in life: terrible movies (like *Cannibal the Musical*) and the threat of global warming. He successfully combines both these passions by producing some of the worst movies in the history of cinema and by marketing an underarm deodorant called Troma Du Aroma which apparently reduces the danger of global warming as well as preventing B.O. Employees of Troma Films wear it all the time.

Later, Jason introduces me to a friend called Glasgow. Glasgow has recently completed what sounds like a promising first short entitled *The Sound of One Hand Clapping*. He gives me a video to watch at my hotel. It's about a man dressed as a Trappist monk who defends himself against nameless karate killers by using his penis as a machine-gun. Jason likes it so much he's thinking of making an exception and putting it in his festival.

FRIDAY, 17 APRIL, LOS ANGELES

Wake up to the sun shining over the Pacific. Every day it does this. Every day the sun shines over the fucking Pacific. Don't they all get sick of it? I've only been here a week and I'm already sick of it.

Tessa has been talking to my old friend Cassian Elwes. Cassian, you will remember, is the guy who screwed up my pitch three years ago over breakfast. He's the you've-got-sausage-on-your-face guy. For three years, I've been looking forward to a return match. Now, I hear, he's out of town. Things will have to wait until Cannes. Meanwhile, he's told Tessa to meet a director called James Merendino. 'You'll love him,' he said to her. 'He gives great TV.'

James lives with his girlfriend in a house near the Hollywood sign. He's thirty-one and drives a clapped-out, bashed-up old Sixties Firebird, which does about three miles to the gallon and looks like it's been rescued from a salvage dump. 'I dropped a new engine in a year ago,' he says, 'and now it runs like shit.' He has a thin face, sticky-up hair, wears ancient clothes and smokes full-strength Marlboros like there's no tomorrow. (He wouldn't get far in my hotel.) He is nothing

90

like anybody I have ever met in LA. To date, he's made seven movies. They have titles like *Livers Ain't Cheap* and *Witchcraft Four*. His latest film, just finished, is called *SLC Punk*, a comedy about punks living in Salt Lake City in the Eighties.

'I didn't know there were any punks living in Salt Lake City,' I say.

'Yes, there were,' he says. 'There was me.'

I like James immediately. He's funny, entertaining, has bags of energy and talks like he's permanently on speed, the words tumbling out in a rich, crazy, adrenaline-charged, nicotine-fuelled rush. He sounds a bit like Quentin Tarantino, his conversation littered with references to pop culture, pulp movies, Big Macs, Quarter-Pounders, on-the-shelf actors, crap TV shows, obscure rock bands, *shlock* comics, other directors (all worse than him) and – Harvey Weinstein. *Harvey Weinstein*? I prick up my ears.

'Have you met him?' I ask.

'Yeah. Once.' He pauses for a nanosecond. 'You know what I'd like to do most of all in Cannes? I'd like to get Harvey to punch me on the nose.'

'You would? Maybe we could, er, you know, film you doing that?'

'Just tell me when you're ready,' says James.

James got into movies when he was seven. He started with Super 8 shorts shot in his parents' backyard ('I nearly burnt the house down once,' he says, 'experimenting'). He made his first 'real' movie when he was 20. Since then he's begged, borrowed, cajoled, threatened and charmed anyone and everyone to put money into his movies. These include Mafia organisations, right-wing fanatics, born-again Christians and soft-porn entrepreneurs. 'The porn guys were the worst,' he says. 'They kept saying, "We want more sex! Put more sex in! There's not enough sex!" Every time they said that, I took the sex out. Just to fuck them off. I ended up making an erotic thriller with absolutely no sex in it at all.'

He lights up another fag. 'You know,' he tells me, 'it's hard getting these guys interested. They know *nothing* about movies. They say, "What's your movie about?" I say, "Well, you know, it's kind of like Kurosawa." They say, "Hiroshima? Didn't we bomb that?"'

SLC Punk is a new departure for James. Unlike his other movies, it's got some big Hollywood figures behind it. It's got Jan de Bont, the director of *Speed*, it's got Michael Peyser, *Speed*'s producer, it's got Beyond Films, the sales agents behind *Strictly Ballroom*. And it's going to Cannes. Five screenings, all in the Market, a huge sales drive, a massive opening night party.

'The party?' says James. 'Well, my producers don't know this, but I'm gonna invite some kids from Marseilles, you know, street kids, just to stir things up a little, maybe tip over the caviar table, smash some furniture, set fire to the place —'

'You want to cause a riot in Cannes?'

'Absolutely. The idea is absolutely to cause a riot in Cannes, yes.'

'Isn't James a perfect pet?' says his girlfriend afterwards.

Three hours later, I get up to leave. I feel exhilarated, elated, excited. James, baby, *I love you!* This is the story I've been waiting for. Nobody has seen *SLC Punk* yet. The first time the industry will get to see it is in Cannes. Everything rides on it. It's James's signature movie. If they love it, he's made. If they hate it, he's dead.

Either way, I win.

We agree to meet tomorrow. James is shooting a TV drama in downtown LA. I will film him there. As I leave he says, 'I've just had a great idea. You know what you ought to do? You ought to put Harvey Weinstein in your movie.'

SATURDAY, 18 APRIL, LOS ANGELES

Wake up to the sun shining over the Pacific. I love it when it does that. Who wants to live in England?

A quick breakfast with Tessa in my hotel. She did have a producer lined up for me this morning but unfortunately he's cancelled. According to Tessa, who has inside knowledge of these things, he was rushed to hospital last night with a vibrator wedged up his bottom. The rumour is, either he or somebody else (who?) pushed it in so deep it got stuck. Tessa says the vibrator was still switched on and buzzing away. (How does she *know* these things?) The doctors decided it was too dangerous to operate until the battery had run out, by which time I suppose the guy must have had about a hundred orgasms. Tessa is clearly very excited about the whole thing, but it puts me completely off my breakfast. I don't think I want to meet him now.

This afternoon, I take a taxi all the way to downtown Los Angeles to meet James Merendino. This is about a 15-mile drive from my hotel in Santa Monica. It takes an hour to find a taxi driver prepared to take me. Nobody ever goes to downtown LA. It used to be the poshest part of the city. Then everybody moved to Hollywood and it became a slum. Now everybody's moved from Hollywood to Beverly Hills and Hollywood's a slum. In a few years' time, Beverly Hills will be a slum and everybody will move back to downtown LA. And so it goes on. I rather like downtown LA. It's about the only part of this characterless city that's got any character. The buildings must be at least 30 years old. The only people who live here now are illegal Mexican immigrants and crack addicts. There are no police cars to be seen, principally because the police are too terrified to go anywhere near the place. The only police I see are fake ones, and they're all in James Merendino's movie.

Right now, he's shooting in an ancient, rotting hotel which looks exactly like the set for *Barton Fink*. It's a huge behemoth of a building, with slimy carpets, peeling wallpaper, filthy windows and rats. It's run by crackheads for other crackheads and also for film-makers like James Merendino in search of the authentic ruin. The film-makers get rid of all the crackheads and replace them with actors pretending to be crackheads whom they then film. (The long arm of Equity reaches even out here, to downtown LA.) An actor posing as a dealer rides with me to the twelfth floor, where James is shooting. The whole floor has been taken over (all the regulars have been kicked downstairs) and is chock full of camera equipment, make-up artists, costume designers, actors, extras, lights and all the rest of the paraphernalia that goes into making movies. James says hi. We're great buddies now. I say, 'What an amazing place. It looks just like the set for *Barton Fink*.'

'That's because it was the set for *Barton Fink*, you ignorant *shmuck*.'

I watch James direct a scene. Somebody once said, the first time you ever visit a movie set is the most exciting day of your life. The second time is the most boring. This is my thousandth time. I expect to be bored rigid, but the peculiar thing is I'm not. An air of excitement – almost of danger – grips this set. James is obviously in his element. Actors, cameraman, crew – everyone is focused, everything is charged with a sense of purpose. Very few directors are able to achieve this and James is one of them. (I'm not.) He leads from the front and his enthusiasm is infectious. I feel it too.

An hour later we're in the vintage Firebird, clattering and

banging and polluting the freeway back to his house. The talk turns to Cannes. 'The thing about Cannes,' says James, 'is that it's not about movies. It's about fish.'

'Fish?'

'It's a fish market,' he informs me. 'You know? I'm taking my fish to the market to see if people think it smells OK.'

'What happens if they don't like the smell?'

'Then,' says James, 'I'm in a little bit of trouble.'

I ask him if he's nervous.

'Nervous? The first screening I'll be nervous. I won't watch it, though. I'll stand outside and smoke a hundred cigarettes and yell and swear at anybody who comes out. I hate screenings. Every time somebody coughs I want to fucking kill them.'

He lights up another fag.

'You know, one time I had a screening and they wouldn't let me in. The guy at the door he said, "Who the hell are you? Don't you know this is a private screening?" I said, "I'm the director." He said, "Yeah, well, you know what? I'm Bruce Willis. Now fuck off."'

Back at James's house, he shows me the first ten minutes of *SLC Punk*. It's slick, it's fast and incredibly noisy. 'I got sixty-two soundtracks in this movie,' he yells over one of them. 'Dontcha just love punk rock?'

No, I think. I hate it.

'Oh, yes,' I say. 'I *love* it.'

Our relationship is still at the delicate stage.

I ask how long it took him to write the script.

'Three days,' he says.

'*Three* days?'

'Yeah. I don't fuck around. I got ten scripts sitting here ready to go. My next is called *Theodore and the Impenetrable Suit of Armour.* Great title, right? It's about a guy who goes to Europe in search of meaninglessness and ends up finding meaning. Existentialism, I love it. I met that guy, whassisname, Samuel Beckett once. He was into all that stuff too. Watch this bit. It's fucking *hilarious.* You know, I love this movie so much I couldn't have made it better myself.'

I wish I felt this way about my movies.

We part well after midnight. At the door, James asks, 'How many therapists have you had in your life?'

'One.'

'I've had twenty.' He says this like I'm supposed to congratulate him. 'Making movies, it's a sickness. You got to be crazy to do this job. One day I'm sure they'll discover the gene that causes it. And when they do I'll take the medication and then I'll be cured. Maybe I'll become an accountant.'

He slaps me on the shoulder.

'See you in Cannes,' he says.

Sunday, 19 April, Los Angeles – New Orleans

Up at five a.m. for the airport. I'm off to New Orleans, to meet a producer called Steve Greenstein. In the taxi I read an article in the *LA Times* about a guy on death row. Two hours before he was due to be executed he developed a terrible headache. The prison doctor examined him, took his temperature, measured his blood pressure, felt his pulse and gave him a couple of painkillers. Then they shot him through the head. I once wrote a script a bit like this, about a guy on death row who demands an impossibly elaborate dish for his last meal. Since this is America, the prison authorities are legally obliged to fulfil his request. The dish is so complicated that they never actually get around to executing him. Now they shoot a guy through the head two hours after curing his headache. What is it with this country?

Steve Greenstein picks me up at the airport. Tessa found him several weeks ago and said I ought to meet him. I'm not sure why. But it's not my money and anyway this is New Orleans so I'm not complaining. Steve looks a bit like John Belushi. He's fat, he's forty, he's balding, he smokes Havana cigars, he drives a red Mercedes convertible and he wears sun-glasses all the time (even at night). He has five mobile phones in the car. For some reason he calls himself 'The Commander'. Every time one of the phones rings he says, 'Commander Hotline go ahead I'm listenin'.' Two minutes into the journey he starts telling me how one of his ex-girl-friends is a registered psychopath intent on murdering him with an axe. Before I'm able to ask why, the phone rings. It takes him a couple of minutes to work out which one. By the time he's finished, he's forgotten what he was telling me. By the time he remembers, the phone rings again. In this way, the conversation continues until we reach our hotel.

'Go get yourself ready,' he says. 'We're going out.'

'Where to?'

'Just leave that to The Commander,' says The Commander. 'But don't think about gettin' any sleep.'

Ten minutes later we're back in the car.

'Why do you wear sunglasses all the time?' I ask.

'They're not sunglasses,' says Steve. 'They just *look* like sunglasses. In fact, they're infrared, high-intensity, night-vision goggles. I got them from a friend in the CIA.'

We hit the old French Quarter. This is supposed to be the glamorous heart of New Orleans, packed with hundreds of jazz clubs. Instead, it seems to be packed with hundreds of tawdry discos and topless dancing bars. We end up in a series of these, every one sleazier than the last. At each, various girls come up to Steve and drape themselves over him. They all say, 'Hey Commander, how ya doin'?'

He says, 'Hey baby, meet Steve. He's from England. He's making a film all about me.'

I try to have a serious conversation about the Cannes Film Festival but this isn't an easy thing to do when you've got a giant pair of tits in your face.

And so it goes on until dawn. I never actually find out what exactly Steve Greenstein has to do with the movie industry, or Cannes, or my documentary.

The sun is rising over the city when he drops me off at my hotel. 'You just call me when you want to start filming. Anything you want, I'm ready. Nothing's too much for The Commander. Those babes, weren't they something? Got to go now. It's my turn to take the kids to school.'

MONDAY, 20 APRIL, NEW ORLEANS – NEW YORK

To the airport. Next stop New York. Steve Greenstein is consigned to history. He's out, finished, in the dustbin, *kaput.* His fifteen minutes will just have to wait. My problem isn't with him, it's with Tessa. Has she gone mad?

New York. The rain sweeps across the city, the clouds so low I can't see the tops of the skyscrapers. I haven't seen any rain for a week. It feels good, as it feels good to be back. I love this city. This is where I first fell in love, where I first had a job, where I first got mugged. (The mugger had an enormous bull whip and he chased me all the way down Eighth Avenue.)* Is it really fifteen years ago? We pass the building where I used to work, a radio station which churned out horrible cheap phone-ins day after day. It was called WMCA ('Your Conversation Station'). I notice it's still there.

To my absolute amazement, I also notice a man I recognise standing outside in the rain, singing at the top of his voice. He was here fifteen years ago, doing exactly the same thing. Day after day, whatever the weather, he would belt out arias, holding out a little cup for people to put money in. Nobody ever did. He knew the words of every opera ever written, he could do the whole *Ring* cycle from start to finish, playing all the parts, never once pausing for breath. His only problem was he couldn't sing. He had a terrible voice. Once we interviewed him for the radio. He spoke so quickly that he was completely unintelligible. We had to slow down the tape to quarter speed before we could understand him. I remember he said opera was the greatest love of his life. He also said he was waiting to be discovered.

I pass him now, standing out in the rain without an umbrella, the empty tumbler still in his hand, a ragged, unshaven, half-crazy, half-inspired figure in an ancient overcoat singing his head off. It looks like he's still waiting.

The image haunts me all night. In one sense, a reassuring link with the past. In another, a bad omen for the future. But which?

---

* This really did happen. I even have witnesses to prove it.

99

TUESDAY, 21 APRIL, NEW YORK

To the offices of Troma, the company run by Lloyd Kaufman which produces fantastic numbers of fantastically awful B movies at fantastically low prices. Kaufman is the guy who picked up *Killer Condom* and *Cannibal the Musical*. A poster of *Cannibal* sits on somebody's desk. It describes it as 'the first intelligent musical about cannibalism'. The offices are incredibly dingy, like a series of student digs. We're a long way from Los Angeles now. Every spare bit of shelf space is stacked with plastic models from Troma's horror movies. There are monsters, blood-sucking freaks, Dracula look-alikes and loads of killer condoms. These are absolutely fearsome. No way would I ever put one on. I think about nicking one and sticking it in my bag (it would make a great anniversary present) but I'm interrupted by a secretary. She gives me a Troma press pack which contains a list of their latest titles. If nothing else, they should win an Oscar for Best Titles. They include (in alphabetical order):

Blondes Have More Guns
Chopper Chicks in Zombie Town
Class of Nuke 'Em High
Class of Nuke 'Em High 2
Class of Nuke 'Em High 3
Demented Death Farm Massacre
Dialing for Dingbats
Hands Up Amigo
I Was a Teenage TV Terrorist
Killer Babe for the CIA
Maniac Nurses Find Ecstasy
Pterodactyl Woman from Beverly Hills
Rabid Grannies
Stuff Stephanie in the Incinerator

'*Stuff Stephanie in the Incinerator* is my personal favourite,' says the secretary, a serious girl in glasses. 'With *Chopper Chicks in Zombie Town* a close second. Would you like a cup of tea?'

A few minutes later, Lloyd's personal assistant comes in. 'Have you seen the press pack?' she asks. 'The thing you've got to understand about Lloyd is he's the greatest living genius since Orson Welles. Did you know *Maniac Nurses Find Ecstasy* has been compared to *Citizen Kane?*'

'No.'

'Yeah, well it has. Lloyd told me himself. Have they given you a cup of tea yet?'

The extraordinary thing about all the people who work for Troma is that they're really serious. And not just about their movies. The assistant asks me if I'd like to sample some Troma Du Aroma, the underarm deodorant devised by Lloyd in order to combat the effects of both global warming and smelly armpits.

'Does it work?' I ask.

'Are you *kidding?*' she says. 'If everybody bought this stuff we'd solve the ozone problem in a week.' (If everybody bought this stuff, Lloyd Kaufman would be a billionaire.)

'You know,' she goes on, 'Lloyd runs a global warming conference every year at Cannes. It's the highlight of the Festival. Here, read this.' She thrusts a press release across the desk. It's about two of Troma's latest movies, due to be premièred in Cannes. It says, 'Regarding the hot topic of Global Warming, Troma is proud to première two very important new films. *Sucker* deals with the burning issues of how Global Warming affects the daily lives of Vampires . . . *Decampitated* is a heart-wrenching study of the effect that massive deforestation has had on libidinous teenage campers and the psychopathic urges of an environmentally conscious serial killer and also has lots of sex and violence . . .'

Lloyd Kaufman, when I meet him, looks alarmingly like my mad opera singer. For one terrible moment, I think he's actually the same person. He speaks very fast and his singing voice is an absolute disgrace. (I know this because he sings me the title music for *Demented Death Farm Massacre*. Or maybe that's how it's supposed to sound.)

He tells me all about his latest movie, which he directed, *Tromeo & Juliet*. All the dialogue is in iambic pentameters. 'It's my best work,' he says. 'Did you know I've been compared to Orson Welles?'

'I did.'

'Look. I'm not knocking Orson. He was good. Fat, but good. But *Tromeo & Juliet* . . . Have you seen the posters?' He hands one over. Under the title, it says: 'Body Piercing. Kinky Sex. Dismemberment. The Things that Made Shakespeare Great.'

Half an hour later I exit Lloyd's office complete with a couple of suitcases full of press releases, catalogues, posters, rubber monsters, a video of *Stuff Stephanie in the Incinerator* . . . and a killer condom. The only problem is going to be getting it through Customs.

TUESDAY, 21 APRIL, HEATHROW AIRPORT

I can keep the video but not the condom. The Customs officer is not convinced when I tell him it's a prop for a movie. He looks at me with distaste and types my name on a computer. From now on, I'm a watched man.

THURSDAY, 23 APRIL, LONDON

This afternoon, Mike Hakata takes me on a guided tour of his fridge. This contains:

    1 Standard 8mm clockwork camera (broken)
    4 rolls of Standard 8mm film
    5 rolls of unexposed 16mm film (sell-by date 2.3.92)
    2 cans of 16mm film containing a pop promo which
    he hasn't got the money to edit yet but hopefully will
    one day
    1 loaf of bread (stale)
    4 eggs (rotten)
    300 duty-free Marlboro Lights
    1 35mm film can containing a half-eaten pizza
    1 lb of what looks at first sight like a mature Stilton
    but in fact turns out to be cheddar

Nineteen days to go. The balance sheet so far: Mike Hakata and James Merendino. That's it. There's nobody else. Hannah is scouring all her contacts in a last-ditch effort to find more characters. I may go to Germany next week for one more try. I am not optimistic. To run this film with only two stories is potentially disastrous. And time is running out. Instead of getting on with the job, I spend the days looking for ways to escape. There *must* be some way out of this mess.

FRIDAY, 24 APRIL, LONDON

Last night I decided to use my six-year-old daughter's potty in order to measure exactly how much I am urinating. Every time I pee, it's like the Niagara Falls. This morning the potty

103

is overflowing, thereby confirming my fears that something is definitely very wrong with my bladder. I am obviously extremely ill. Even Sally says how pale I look. There is clearly little chance of my recovering in time to make this film. I expect I'll just have to spend the whole of the Cannes Film Festival in bed, with a hot-water bottle.

Tonight I stagger across London to meet Mike and his producer Rolf for a drink. They are joined by Peter Johnston. Peter comes from Northern Ireland and describes himself as a publicity terrorist. He used to run an underground newspaper in Belfast called *DV8* which was banned after he stuck a Union Jack on the cover in the colours of the Irish flag. Now he's been hired by Rolf to promote *Two Bad Mice* in Cannes. Peter takes his job very seriously. Unlike most film publicists, he wears combat gear on the job and operates only at night. He has an entire arsenal of spray paints at his disposal. He is especially excited about one particular new product which is absolutely impossible to erase. He intends to spray-paint the whole of Cannes with it. This includes cars, walls, pavements, shop windows, restaurant fronts, other movie posters, plus the newly refurbished lobby of the Carlton Hotel. Peter also plans to go around Cannes stamping people's foreheads with the title of Mike's film. Here again, the dye is almost impossible to remove, which means that a large proportion of major movie executives will probably spend the whole of next year with the words TWO BAD MICE printed on their foreheads. For this there's always the chance he'll spend three or four days in prison. 'It all comes with the job,' he says.

If the BBC employed people like this, we wouldn't ever have to worry about budgets again.

SATURDAY, 25 APRIL, LONDON

Hannah has asked me to meet Stephen Loyd, a minicab driver who has written a script called *Amsterdam*. She says it's about a bunch of lads who head off to a dope festival in Amsterdam and smoke themselves unconscious on a giant bong called The Lord. I ask her what a bong is and she looks at me like I'm the owner of a Retired Person's Bus Pass. (Apparently, it's a four-foot bit of drainpipe used to inhale cannabis – so now I know.) Stephen is 29 and lives in Leytonstone, East London. His gut is not a pretty sight. Despite the fact it's freezing outside, he's wearing white socks, sandals, bermuda shorts and an Hawaiian shirt. I think he thinks this makes him look like a glamorous film producer. It doesn't.

Over several beers (his not mine) Stephen describes how he wrote *Amsterdam* while doing nights in the minicab. 'I've written it phonetically, because I can't fucking spell,' he says. 'It's about a bunch of lads who go to Amsterdam for this annual dope festival. One of them's called Rupert, he's the nerd of the gang, and he stones himself unconscious on the biggest spliff in the world.'

'You mean like . . . a giant bong,' I interject.

'Yeah. Right. A giant bong.' Stephen looks at me with sudden respect. 'Anyway. As a result he spends the entire time in a coma. His friends invent this whole history for him – you know, shagging loads of birds and stuff – so that when he wakes up he thinks he's a hero. Then he finds out the truth.'

'Is it based on personal experience?'

'Yeah, sort of. Except it wasn't Amsterdam, exactly. It was Margate.'

Stephen's idea is to take his script to Cannes. The goal is

to raise £1.2 million to make the film. Going with him is his director, Gordon Mason, and an associate called Spooky. Spooky is an ex-nightclub bouncer with broken teeth and a newly discovered interest in acting. He's hoping to have a part in the movie, if it ever gets made. His role in Cannes is a little unclear, except he's apparently willing to get himself arrested or deported in order to help sell the script. Meanwhile, accreditation has already been sorted since Stephen knows a friend who knows another friend who happens to be an expert forger. Likewise, transport has been arranged. To travel the 868 miles from Leytonstone to Cannes, Stephen has borrowed an ex-British Telecom banana-yellow van with a dodgy clutch, no tax disc, no MOT, no brakes, a duff speedometer and a giant spliff leaf painted on each side.

'We've got AA Five Star Insurance,' says Stephen. 'In case we crash.'

Stephen reckons it will take three days to get to Cannes. He's already prepared a detailed inventory for the van. This includes: three sleeping bags, 2000 stickers (to advertise the film), 80 copies of the script, 1400 leaflets, 50 tins of baked beans and a tin opener. All three of them will sleep in the back. That's if they don't end up killing each other.

I ask if he's ever been to France before.

'Once,' he replies, 'when I was eleven. It was a school trip. We went over on the ferry, spent an hour or two pissing off the locals, came home on the ferry. So yeah, I've been to France before.'

'How are you going to get people to read the script?'

'We'll use the handcuffs.'

'*Handcuffs?*'

'Yeah. Anybody comes past who looks important, we handcuff him. Then we bundle him in the back of the van, show him the script. He says how much do you need, we tell him £1.2 million, he puts the money in and we give him a lift back to his hotel. Simple as that, see? Spooky can do the handcuffs, he's good at that sort of thing. Plus he don't mind getting nicked. I'm thinking maybe that bloke Harvey Weinstein ought to see the script. You know him?'

'Not personally,' I say.

Stephen asks if I could lend him a picture of Harvey so he doesn't handcuff the wrong person by mistake.

At the end of the Festival Stephen intends to set fire to the van (if possible right in front of the Carlton Hotel) in order to collect the insurance and fly home on Easyjet.

On Monday I meet Gordon. I walk home on air. We are definitely back in business.

SUNDAY, 26 APRIL, LONDON

On location with Mike Hakata. He's making another movie. The budget for this one is £500. We're in Notting Hill and it's raining. Mike is doing a murder scene. The killer uses a cap gun. It makes a little pop every time it fires. Mike says he'll add the sound effects later, if he can persuade his mum's boyfriend to lend him the money.

I go round the set asking everybody (a) what they think of Mike, (b) what they think of the film and (c) how much they're getting paid. The answers, in every case, are (a) he's mad (b) no comment and (c) nothing. Everybody says they're in it for love, except one person who says he had nothing better to do on a rainy Sunday afternoon so he thought he might as well come out and make a movie.

At one point the shoot is threatened by a group of toughs from the local estate who keep making catcalls every time the actors say their lines. Then they try to smash the camera. One of the actors threatens them with the cap gun, at which point I suddenly remember an urgent appointment on the other side of London and promptly leave without saying good-bye.

Tonight, as I am putting her to bed, my six-year-old daughter says, 'Daddy, just what *exactly* is your film about?' I am at a loss for words.

MONDAY, 27 APRIL, LONDON

My doctor says my wee problem is the result of chronic hysterical psychosis due to prolonged stress. I say, I suppose that means a major operation, then? No, she says, it means a couple of aspirin a day. I will have to get a second opinion.

Over to Leytonstone to meet Stephen Loyd and Gordon Mason, his director. Gordon is a film editor with his own company, Headflicks. *Amsterdam* will be his first feature. Gordon originally got interested in films when he was at school. From what I can gather, this was a 'progressive' institution, which meant that it was run by a bunch of hippies out of their heads on acid. A visit to the headmaster usually meant sharing a joint with him in his study. I find Stephen and Gordon at the Millennium Café, a foul-smelling greasy spoon in Leytonstone. A dense fog of cannabis smoke hangs over their table. Gordon is clearly spaced out of his mind and his eyes roll alarmingly in his skull. He says *Amsterdam* isn't the only film he's working on. He's also directing a documentary, which he's hoping to sell in Cannes.

'What's the title?' I ask.

'*They Call It Acid*,' says Gordon, and his eyes roll round and round in his head until I start to get dizzy.

Gordon tells me the reason he likes *Amsterdam* so much is because you can read it without a dictionary. 'It's a really brilliant script,' he asserts. 'Except for all the bits which don't make sense.'

'Yeah, but that's only about ten per cent,' says Stephen.

'And the spelling is crap.'

'Yeah, but that's because I can't fucking spell.'

'Otherwise it's perfect.'

Gordon blows a huge cloud of cannabis smoke in my face.

'We've never been to Cannes before,' he says. (He pronounces it Cans as in baked beans.) 'So we don't know how it works. I mean, do you just walk down Cannes High Street and sort of ask people for £1.2 million?'

'No, first we handcuff them. Then we ask for £1.2 million,' Stephen explains.

'I've been practising my pitch,' says Gordon. 'I've got a five-minute version, a three-minute version, a one-minute version and a thirty-second version.'

'What's the thirty-second version?'

'Five guys go to Amsterdam . . . is it five or six?'

'Five,' Stephen confirms. 'You're supposed to be the fucking director.'

'Five guys go to Amsterdam for the weekend, go to a dope festival, get really out of it, get into all sorts of trouble, have a laugh, have a fight, get the ferry back, get off the ferry and get arrested for the garage they've robbed to raise the money to go there in the first place. How long was that?'

'One minute sixteen seconds.'

'Too long, isn't it?' asks Gordon. 'I'll have to get it down.'

Afterwards, they show me the van. It looks like it's been dredged up from the bottom of the sea. There are holes in the roof, in the floor, in the sides. 'Isn't it a beauty?' says Stephen, proudly. He kicks a wheel and the hub falls off. ''Course it needs a bit of work here and there. We're going to paint it banana yellow. The spliff leaf goes here.' He points at the side. 'It's going to be four foot high, five foot wide, with AMSTERDAM — A VERY BRITISH COMEDY in great big green Seventies bubble writing on the top. What do you reckon?'

'It's . . . terrific,' I say.

'You'd have to be Ray fucking Charles or Stevie Wonder not to notice that,' says Stephen.

TUESDAY, 28 APRIL, LONDON

Stephen has been showing me one of his old school reports. This is from Henry Compton Miller School in Fulham. He was 15 at the time. It is, without any question, the worst school report I have ever seen. Stephen is very proud of it. He reads bits of it to me:

Out of 176 days this term, Stephen was absent 146 days and of the 30 appearances he put in he was late eight times.

English. Stephen has made no effort to take part in English lessons and on the rare occasions he has appeared it is a great pity he has not got himself more organised.

Human Biology. Stephen very rarely bothers to attend human biology.

Music. Usually absent and a nuisance when present.

Technical Drawing. Never seen in class this year.

Design and Technology. The only thing that I can say of Stephen is that he is on the register for Design and Technology. He has attended twice and done nothing on both occasions.

Form Master. Stephen has diligently and enthusiastically avoided school and on his rare appearances managed to avoid any form of participation whatsoever. A commendable achievement.

'I wasn't out nicking car stereos,' says Stephen. 'I was stacking shelves in the local supermarket. I ended up with a social worker who tried to get me to go to school but it didn't work, see? That's why I have problems with spelling.'

'Why have you kept that school report?' I ask.

'Why have I kept it?' He pauses for a moment. 'Because it's the only one I ever got.'

Amsterdam isn't Stephen's first script. 'I've got about ten on the go at the moment,' he says. 'There's *Friend or Foe*, which I'm working on in the cab at the moment, there's *Large*, which is the sequel to *The German Job*, which I sent to Paramount but they weren't interested. There's *Four Maybes and a Relative*, which is the first of two sequels to *Friend or Foe*. There's *Prison Pals*, which I'm about thirty or forty pages through . . .'

'Do you like writing?'

'Well, it's better than driving a cab. What I'd really like to do is distribute the film myself, in a seven-and-a-half-ton truck. Sell off all 184 foreign territories in Cannes, use the money to pay for the distribution to all 557 theatrical outlets in the UK, use the profits from that to bankroll the next movie. That's where the big money is.'

184 territories? 557 theatrical outlets? Where did he learn all this?

'I did the Dov S. Simans Two-Day Film Seminar. Like Quentin Tarantino. Day One, How to Make a Movie. Day Two, How to Sell It.' He lights a giant spliff. 'All this stuff is Day Two.'

'Day Two.'

'That's right. It's the domino effect, see? You just got to get the first one started. Then you're in the money. I mean, Harvey Weinstein, he's no different. Where was he fifteen years ago?'

Afterwards I ask Gordon, 'Do you think Stephen is the next Harvey Weinstein?'

'He's fucking fat enough,' says Gordon.

Wednesday, 29 April, London

Reflecting back on yesterday's meeting, it seems to me I've missed its essence. Got up early this morning to jot down my impressions. Stephen's flat in Leytonstone. The place is falling apart. The paint is peeling off the walls, the carpet is threadbare, the windows opaque with grime. Ashtrays stuffed full of cigarette butts perch on second-hand chairs. A poster of *Withnail and I* hangs askew above the sofa. Stephen asks me if I'd like a coffee and we go into the kitchen next door. In here, there is no paint at all, just bare brickwork, and the sink is piled with a million years of unwashed plates, dishes, saucepans, frying-pans. The room reeks of bacon fat. The milk is off. I ask Stephen if I can film him in the flat. The moment I do I feel ashamed. What am I trying to achieve? This is cheap and I know it's cheap. He refuses and his refusal gives him a kind of dignity, which only underlines its absence in me.

Why did he show me that school report? The question pulled at me while I was with him and it pulls at me now, as I'm writing this. Is it a kind of pride? Is it some sort of grand gesture of rebellion, a big fuck you to the word (and me)? I don't know. What I do know is that this is the closest Stephen has come to opening the door on his past. It hints at a world of broken homes, of social workers, of a school which seems to have given up on him. For Stephen to read that report at all suggests a vulnerability which, I know too well, is very easy to abuse. But what it also suggests is courage, a determination to stand up and be counted, to cross into an entirely alien and unforgiving world – the movie business – and make a mark. Leytonstone to Cannes. Minicab driver to movie-maker. Of course, there are huge comic possibilities here. I'd be an idiot to ignore them. The guy is there, on a plate. The story is wide open, bristling with potential. But there's more, much more, to it than that. Or am I being sentimental?

THURSDAY, 30 APRIL, LONDON

Pascale and I spend the morning thinking titles. I'm not very good at this and neither, it turns out, is she. What we need now is Lloyd Kaufman from Troma Films. We need *Chopper Chicks in Zombie Town*. We need *Stuff Stephanie in the Incinerator*. Instead, we come up with these:

Canned Glory
Citizen Cannes
Cannes Used To Be Glam
No Cannes Do
There's No Film in the Cannes
Cannes Do Cannes Don't
Why do Fools Fall in Cannes
In Cannes No One Can Hear You Scream
Cannes You Think of a Title (Because I Cannes Not)
Hotel du Crap

This takes the whole morning. By the time we get to *Hotel du Crap* we decide it's time to go to the pub. Pascale thinks the only solution is to go through Halliwell's film guide and nick somebody else's title. I'm not sure what the copyright situation is here, but I haven't got a better idea. Actually, I *have* got a better idea, which is why don't we go the whole hog and nick an entire film instead? That way we won't have to do any more work, plus we can put the rest of the budget (£350,000) towards my summer holiday in Bali.

Friday, 1 May, Munich

Ten days to go. Out on the first flight to Munich. Back tonight. Our German executive, Christine Ruppert, is pulling out all the stops to find us a German film-maker. Why won't she just give up and admit defeat? She lines up twenty people for me to see in eight hours. They're all hopeless. I'm annoyed because (a) this is a complete waste of time, (b) time is what we do not have right now and (c) all these executives seem hell-bent on turning this film into some kind of horrible Europudding. If there's one thing I can't stand it's a Europudding. Neither can the audience.

The only bright spot on the horizon is the reappearance of my old friend Hans Horn, winner of last year's Oscar for the World's Most Boring Director. He's clearly still in terrific form and definitely the favourite for next year's Oscar as well. We talk – or rather he talks – for over an hour while I consider asking him whether he'd like to be in the film. Unfortunately, while I am considering, I also fall asleep. When I wake up, Hans Horn has gone.

The single benefit of this trip is that we don't have to put a German in the film any more. We've run through the list. There's nobody left to meet. Even Christine admits defeat. At the very least, that's one less battle to fight.

Christine gives me a lift to the airport. In the terminal, I notice a desk with the sign GEPÄCK (Luggage). Behind it sits a very thin man. Next to him is another desk with the sign GROSS GEPÄCK (Heavy Luggage). Behind it sits an extremely fat man. I wonder whether this is for the benefit of those who don't speak German.

SATURDAY, 2 MAY, LONDON

I'm sitting in Stephen Loyd's minicab outside McDonald's where he's reading me a bit of his script. Or rather, I'm trying to get him to read a bit of his script. For some reason, he's suddenly become extremely shy. It doesn't suit him.

'I hate being in front of the camera,' he says.

'Just read one scene,' I say.

'I'm not an actor.'

'Oh, come on. One teeny weeny scene. I bet it's terrific.'

'Oh, alright then,' he says. 'Pick a number from one to ninety-two.'

'Sixty-three.'

'Sixty-three.' He flips through the pages while I film, camera in one hand, cheeseburger in the other.

'Good choice,' he says.

And then he starts to read.

Two things are immediately apparent. First, Stephen Loyd is correct. He's definitely not an actor. Second, his script is largely unintelligible. At least to me. In fairness, this may have a lot to do with the fact we're starting on page sixty-three and not page one. There's some stuff about Jimmy and Billy and Vince and Colin and Charlie and Killer (not his real name) and there are two German girls and there's that giant bong thing that you smoke through a drainpipe and . . . and . . . and I simply can't make heads or tails of it.

'Well?' asks Stephen, afterwards.

'Just as I thought,' I say. 'Terrific.'

I'm beginning to sound like a movie producer.

This evening I film Stephen buying a pair of handcuffs from a sex shop in Soho. He tries on several pairs, but none of them are strong enough. Finally, he settles on one he thinks will do the job. We leave the shop and I ask him to try it on for size, which he does. 'Nobody's going to get *these* off in a hurry,' he says, waving his wrist at the camera. Then he discovers he's lost the key.

We return to the sex shop where the assistant unlocks the handcuffs and tries to sell him six bottles of amyl nitrate and a pair of patent-leather thigh-high boots at the same time.

I have an awful premonition that Spooky will clamp the

116

handcuffs on Harvey just at the point when Harvey is punching James Merendino on the nose. This would present major logistical complications. It would require a minimum of three cameras, several technicians, a lighting director and up to five production assistants. I suppose the only way to approach the whole thing is to think of it as an Outside Broadcast event, like the Royal Wedding.

MONDAY, 4 MAY, LONDON

I'm standing on a street corner in King's Cross filming Mike Hakata. He's eating fish and chips out of a paper bag. 'We used to wash car windscreens here,' he says. 'A whole posse of us. In fact, we made quite a lot of money. It was great fun. The only problem was all the nutters. King's Cross is fucking full of nutters.'

'Were you living in the hostel at the time?'

'Oh, no. I was living in the back of somebody's van.'

'So what did you spend the money on?'

'Movies.'

Fresh from the editing room (where he's putting the finishing touches to his new movie) Mike is taking me on a guided tour of his past. 'Give me a typical day,' I ask.

'Well,' says Mike, 'I'd get up at six or eleven depending on whether the guy who owned the van needed it that day. Then it was over here, do a couple of hours' windscreens. Then I'd go to see a movie. You know, Renoir, Kurosawa, Truffaut, maybe a Wim Wenders retrospective at the Electric, whatever was on. Then I'd do more car windscreens. Then maybe another movie. Then bed, depending whether the van was back or not. If it wasn't I'd go and see a movie. Once I saw four Jean-Luc Godard movies in one day. *À Bout de Souffle* is definitely one of my all-time favourite films. Do you want a chip?'

An hour later we're outside the hostel where Mike lived for eighteen months. He hasn't been back since he left three years ago. The hostel is in a nondescript terraced house a few yards from King's Cross Station. From the outside, it looks almost attractive, all white stucco and pillars on the door, not what I expected at all. One of the residents watches us curiously.

Mike is obviously uncomfortable. 'Do they know we're coming?' he asks. 'You'd better watch that camera. Take your eye off it for a second and you'll never see it again. Everybody nicks everything in here.'

Inside, the place looks almost like students' digs, again not what I expected. But there are differences. There's a board in the hallway, for instance, with an IN/OUT sign against the name of every resident. ('Every time you wanted to go out, you had to move the sign to OUT,' says Mike, 'so they always knew where you were.') There's a TV set, bolted to the floor, encased in a steel cage. ('It was always getting nicked.') There's a kitchen, with no food on the shelves, in the cupboards or in the fridge. ('That was always getting nicked too.') Everywhere there are posters warning about the dangers of drugs.

'Did you do any drugs?' I ask Mike.

He pauses for a moment. 'Yeah, I did.' Another pause. 'There was a time when getting completely blotto was a major incentive to get out of bed in the morning.'

'What kind of drugs did you do?'

'Anything,' he says. 'Anything and everything. I didn't care. I just didn't care.' He looks around the room. 'God, those were grim days.'

We go upstairs to his old room. A warden unlocks the

door. For a moment, Mike doesn't go in. Or won't. Or can't. He says, 'Bloody hell, it smells the same.' The room is almost bare, a bed in one corner, a table, a cupboard, a lamp hanging from the ceiling. The walls are stained. The air is close and Mike opens the window. 'You go out of your head in here,' he says quietly. 'I used to spend hours and hours in this room, listening to King's Cross buzzing outside the window, thinking got to do something with my life, got to get out of this place.' He sits down on the bed, lights a fag. 'It feels like another world, now.'

I've known Mike for . . . what? . . . six weeks, but I've never known him like this. For several minutes, we sit together in silence. Then he starts to talk about his film, how he wrote the script in this very room. And as he does so the life returns to his voice. He becomes animated, energetic and, for an instant, I see why it is that Mike makes movies. Watching the rushes later, I see this even more clearly: a visible, almost tangible possession of his mind by his passion, where all the brain-numbing depression and sense of failure are suddenly replaced by something else — self-respect, perhaps, or hope. I've met hundreds of film-makers from all over the world, but I've never seen this feeling — this reason for doing what they do — so forcefully expressed. In the end, I suppose, Mike speaks for all of them. Perhaps for me too, despite the fact that my life was never like his life.

'I remember once, being on location,' says Mike. 'I was living in the hostel at the time and I was directing this night shoot. You've got to imagine. It's freezing cold, four a.m., everyone's exhausted, the lights aren't working, the money's running out, there are definite feelings of mutiny in the air, nobody's getting paid a fucking penny — and I'm standing there with a styrofoam cup of cold coffee in my hand thinking, *what have I done?* I'm responsible for all this and it's going to be fucking *terrible*. And then along comes my cameraman, and he says, "OK, Mike, we're ready to go." And it's like, suddenly action everywhere. Lights, actors, people running around, turnover, clap the board, action, *we're off*! And I remember thinking, God I love this. I absolutely love it. This is what I was put on earth to do.'

We return downstairs.

'Do you think', I ask, 'you could end up back here, if it all goes wrong?'

He looks at me. 'Never,' he says. 'Even if it all goes wrong in Cannes, even if nobody wants to buy my movie, even if I end up making movies for fifty quid for the rest of my life, I am never coming back here. As sure as I know the sun will rise tomorrow, I know I am never coming back to this place.'

Outside, we say good-bye. Mike goes to Cannes in two weeks. I won't see him until then. He shakes my hand and walks away. My sound recordist turns to me and says, 'Fucking great interview that,' a comment which, though true, leaves me with a bitter taste in the mouth.

Afterwards, in the office, Hannah and Pascale watch the rushes. 'Very nice,' says Pascale. 'Although it's a pity it doesn't look more like . . . a *real* hostel. Don't you think?'

TUESDAY, 5 MAY, LONDON

An eleventh-hour meeting with Pascale and my terrifyingly efficient production manager, Brian, to discuss last-minute logistics. Everything is in place. This is the line-up: two 16mm film crews, one Super 8mm cameraman, two mini video cameras, four production assistants, one production secretary, one researcher, one producer – and me. Sixteen people in all. It's a massive unit, far bigger – and potentially far more unwieldy – than anything I am used to. Communication is going to be a nightmare. We've all been issued mobile phones, but I happen to know that last year the entire mobile phone system in Cannes broke down because 25,000 movie producers were all on their mobile phones at the same time. 'Oh, we'll manage,' says Brian helpfully, but we won't and he knows it and I know he knows it. We're following three film-makers – Mike, Stephen and James – all of whom will be doing different things in different places at the same time. How do we cover it?

'Ah,' says Brian, 'I've thought of that. Have a look at *this*.' He pushes a piece of paper across the table. Every square inch is covered with hundreds of unintelligible squiggles, arrows, boxes, circles, letters, numbers, all joined up by lots of lines. It looks like a circuit diagram for a giant super-computer.

'What is it?' I ask.

'It's the production schedule,' states Brian proudly. 'I spent hours doing that.'

'Oh. What does it mean?'

'It means', says Brian, 'that nothing can possibly go wrong. Stick to this and we won't sink.'

'That's what they said about the *Titanic*.'

'They did?' asks Brian. 'I haven't seen it yet.'

The more I look at it, the more I panic. Two crews working a shift pattern of fourteen hours a day. That covers the whole twenty-four.

'Of course, we can't ask the crews to work more than fourteen hours,' says Brian. 'They'd mutiny.'

'But what about me?' I ask.

'What about you?'

'I'm supposed to be the director. That means you're expecting me to direct – twenty-four hours a day.'

'Well, not *every* day.'

'When am I supposed to sleep?'

'You don't. You're the director.' He stuffs the production schedule back into his briefcase. 'I suppose if push comes to shove you can always use my shower.'

We move on to discuss the cast. Pascale says, 'It's too Anglocentric.' What does she mean, *Anglocentric?*

'What do you mean, Anglocentric?' I ask.

'Everybody speaks English.'

'What's wrong with that?'

'The trouble with you, Stephen,' she says, 'is that you think small. Small is everyone in this film speaking English. I think big. Big is someone in this film not speaking English.'

'You're saying I'm a Eurosceptic?'

'I'm saying we need a foreigner.'

'But we've only got *six days.*'

'I know,' admits Pascale. Then she drops her bombshell. 'That's why you're coming with me to Paris. Tomorrow. We're going to meet a man called Erick Zonca.'

'Erick *who?*'

WEDNESDAY, 6 MAY, PARIS

The instant I meet Erick Zonca I just know we're not going to get on. First, he's very handsome. Second, he's suave, sophisticated and French. Third, he's meant to be unbelievably talented. Fourth, he's infinitely more successful than me. Fifth, he's got a full head of hair. Sixth, he's also extremely nice.

On the other hand, he and Pascale get on famously. This is partly because she speaks French and I don't (well, I'm *Anglocentric*), partly because they're able to swap endless gossip about lots of other French directors I've never heard of.

Erick Zonca is in his early forties and he's just finished his first feature film, *La Vie Revée des Anges* (*The Dreamlife of Angels*). It's taken him three years. Last December, as a kind of joke, he sent a rough cut to Gilles Jacob, head of the Cannes Film Festival, the man who decides the line-up for the Competition. Gilles Jacob has been around for decades – he virtually *is* the Cannes Film Festival. In his time he's discovered directors like Jean-Luc Godard, Louis Malle, François Truffaut and a whole host of others. To be blessed by Gilles Jacob is a sure step on the road to fame, glory and riches. This, of course, is exactly what didn't happen to Mike Hakata. His movie was rejected. But it's exactly what did happen to Erick Zonca. Not only did Jacob accept his movie, he *loved* his movie and he even asked to see it again, this time with Erick, just because he loved it so much. From this point on, the story becomes a sort of fairy-tale, in which Erick Zonca is poised to become the toast of Cannes, hailed by the world as the new Godard, the next Truffaut, the French answer to Ken Loach, Quentin Tarantino, Orson Welles, Roberto Rossellini, all wrapped up in one. This, of course, is a fairy-tale I'm very familiar with because exactly the same thing has happened to me too, and more than once. The only difference between me and Erick is that I always wake up.

It's all wonderfully exciting stuff, of course, except for one problem. Erick doesn't want to be in our film. What's he talking about? *Everybody* wants to be in our film. All over Britain, Germany, Ireland, the United States, people are begging, pleading, going down on their hands and knees to be in our film. (I'd want to be in it if I didn't have to bloody make it.) This is *showbusiness*, for God's sake, where everybody is horribly vain, conceited, self-important, arrogant, egomaniacal – and desperate.

123

I suppose that's the key. Erick Zonca is not desperate. He doesn't need us. We need him. 'I hate Cannes, anyway,' he says. You have to be a first-time feature film director with a movie selected for the Competition to be able to talk like that. 'For me, it will be arrive, show the movie, depart. Maybe some interviews. This is not interesting for you, I think.'

'Oh, no,' says Pascale. 'It's *extremely* interesting.'

'My answer', he says, 'is no.'

'No?'

'No.'

'OK, then,' I say. 'How much?'

'What?'

'Two thousand. Dollars.'

'Dollars?'

'Pounds.'

'Pounds?'

'Three thousand. Four. Six. Name your price. Anything you want.'

'No.'

Later, back on the Eurostar, Pascale says, 'I've had a word with Erick again. I think he'll do it. For nothing. But there are conditions. He'll let us film only at certain times. No access to his private life. No questions about his family. And you can't interview him in the bath.' (Interviewing people in the bath — theirs, not mine — happens to be one of my specialities.) 'Plus he may pull out at any time.'

'Sounds like a great deal,' I say.

'It's the best we'll get,' she snaps. 'There are too many losers in this film. We need a winner. A star. Plus he's French. French means . . . *Eurocentric.*'

We part at Waterloo.

'You know what,' I say to Pascale, 'I don't think Zonca liked me very much.'

'You know what,' she replies. 'He didn't.'

THURSDAY, 7 MAY, LONDON

In less than a week I'll be in Cannes. My stomach is in knots.
I'm not sleeping at night. I stare at the ceiling and think of
all the billion things that are going to go wrong. I remember
reading somewhere how John Schlesinger used to stop his car
on the way to a shoot in order to be sick out of the window.
I've done this loads of times and I haven't even got to Cannes
yet. Also, I've become very superstitious. For instance: I now
only walk between the lines. (Don't fool me, I *know* the bears
are out there. Half of them are financing this film, the other
half are lining up to slam it when it's done.) If I step on a
line, I have to start all over again. This is something I haven't
done since I was six. My daughter does it too. The difference
is she really is six.

The afternoon is spent with Stephen and Gordon in the
greasy spoon. Their clothes are covered with yellow paint.
'The van's nearly done,' says Stephen. 'It looks lovely. Also,
we've put a new horn in. It goes like this. De de de de de
da da da da. Get it? It's the '"Charge of the Cavalry", see?'

'So everybody will know we're coming,' explains Gordon.

'Who's doing the driving?' I ask.

'I am,' says Stephen.

'He is,' says Gordon.

'We're going to pick up a few crates of beer in Calais. I
don't mind getting a driving ban in France.'

Stephen tells me he's also shot a trailer for *Amsterdam*. 'It
should've been fifteen minutes,' he says, 'but I left the cast
unsupervised in the Hare and Hounds for two hours and
they all got pissed.'

'And the master tapes got nicked,' adds Gordon.

'And the master tapes got nicked. So it's only eight minutes. But otherwise it's OK. People talk about directing like it's something special but it's just point-and-shoot, really. No disrespect to yourself but let's face it, it's a mug's game. My nan could do it. Except she couldn't because she's dead.'

'What do you think of the trailer, Gordon?' I enquire.

'Er . . .'

'It's not a bad trailer,' says Stephen.

'Um . . .'

'It does its job,' says Stephen.

'It does its job,' says Gordon.

'It definitely does its job,' says Stephen.

'But otherwise it's crap.'

Stephen shows me a video of the trailer. Gordon is right. It's crap. The one remarkable thing is that Stephen is in it. He plays a character called Jimmy. Amazingly, Jimmy sounds exactly like Stephen. In one fifteen-second speech, he says the word 'fuck' or 'fucking' twelve times. I know this because Stephen rewinds the tape several times to count them. He calls this game 'Let's Count the Fucks' and he plays it all afternoon. 'Let's count 'em again,' he says.

'I couldn't fucking bear it,' I protest.

'Your trouble', says Stephen, 'is that you swear too much.'

I ask Stephen and Gordon if they're going to take the trailer to Cannes.

'Yes,' says Stephen.

'No,' says Gordon.

'Yes, we will,' says Stephen.

'No, we won't,' says Gordon.

'Will.'

'Won't.'

'Will.'
'Won't.'
'Will.'
'Won't.'

This goes on for several minutes. Afterwards, Gordon says to me, 'I don't know why you want to film me and Steve. All we ever fucking do is argue.'

I know, I think. That's why.

'Do you?' I say. 'That's not at all why.'

On the way to my car, Stephen says, 'You know, you've got a funny way of walking.'

How am I to tell him about the bears?

FRIDAY, 8 MAY, LONDON

Thinking about Stephen and Gordon in bed this morning. We meet again on Sunday. Sunday is the beginning of the shoot, the first day of Principal Photography, the point of no return. Sunday is also the day when Stephen, Gordon and Spooky leave for France. It's agreed I will follow them in another van. I'll also take Hannah, a sound recordist and my Super 8 cameraman. We'll meet up with the rest of the team in Cannes.

A few calculations: Leytonstone to Cannes. That's 868 miles. Stephen expects to get there by Tuesday evening. The Festival starts on Wednesday. The big question is, what happens if they're late? The bigger question is, what happens if they're *really* late, i.e. if they get to Cannes after the end of the Festival? (Actually, I know what happens. They meet a load of dentists.)

If so, what do I do? Do I stay or do I go? Do I take the risk that Stephen and Gordon *not* getting to Cannes is a better story than everyone else *being* there? It's one hell of a risk. It means dumping £150,000 worth of crews and equipment waiting down in Cannes. It means dumping four months of research. It means dumping Mike Hakata, Erick Zonca, James Merendino. All on the off-chance that a road movie with Stephen and Gordon is the better bit. Plus I've been commissioned to make a film about the Cannes Film Festival. Pascale would certainly cut my balls off before she'd let me do it. Then she'd fire me.

And yet . . . I can't get rid of this niggling instinct that something is going to go wrong on the journey to Cannes.

Last afternoon in the office. Hannah has been speaking to Frank and Aaron, the two young producers we met last month. They're still hoping to raise £20m worth of business in Cannes. We agree she should invite them to be in our film. They are our back-up, our insurance policy, if Erick Zonca pulls out. We'll run all five stories to begin with. If Erick stays, they go. Not that we tell them this.

They fly in to Nice next Friday. We arrange for them to take the helicopter to Cannes. This is the most expensive, and the most prestigious, way to arrive. All the big producers go by helicopter. The less big producers go by taxi. The minnows take the bus. Mike Hakata will hitch a lift.

'But', says Frank, 'we'd never normally take the helicopter.'

'So what?' I say. 'It looks better.'

'But it's not true.'

'Look,' I explain. 'This is fly-on-the-wall film-making, right? Who the fuck cares if it's true?'

At six o'clock I leave the office.

Bronwen wishes me luck.

Hannah says, 'See you tomorrow.'
Pascale says, 'See you in Cannes.'
'If we ever get there,' I say.
'If you don't,' she says, 'I'll cut your balls off.'
We both have a jolly good laugh about that.

SATURDAY, 9 MAY, LONDON

Last-minute packing. I've got everything ready. Six bottles of aspirin, four bottles of Extra Strong Panadol, 20 sachets of Sudafed, 20 eight-tablet packets of Distalgesic, three bottles of Valium, four packets of seasickness pills for the ferry, one large bottle of multi-vitamin pills, a case of suppositories, three packets of Diareze in case they're too effective, a tube of Canesten Cream for the eczema on my bottom, five sachets of Beecham's Resolve, and a few clothes.

So here we are, at last. After four months, this finally is *it*. I spend the day feeling sick. My nerves are wound up like a thousand springs. Sally takes me out to lunch but I can't eat. I try to have an afternoon nap but I can't sleep. This is terrible. I feel awful. I feel utterly unprepared. The sick irony is I actually *wanted* to make this film. I did everything I could to make it happen. Everybody says, 'Oh, you must be thrilled,' but I'm not thrilled at all. I'm terrified. Right now, I'd rather do anything than this. I'd rather have a triple bypass.

Eight o'clock. Twelve hours to go. To take my mind off things I call my Auntie Becky to wish her a happy birthday. She's 97 today.

She asks, 'Have you finished that thingybob you're doing on the telly yet?'

'Not exactly, Auntie.'

'Well you'd better hurry up, dear,' she says. 'I'll be dead soon.'

She's not the only one.

ACT II

PRINCIPAL
PHOTOGRAPHY

The Cannes Film Festival

FADE UP:

EXT. CANNES. DAY. THE CROISETTE

A hot afternoon half-way through the Cannes Film Festival. Out on the Croisette, the Blues Brothers are playing tracks from their latest movie, Blues Brothers 2000. *Huge arc lights illuminate a stage which groans under the weight of A list celebrities. Dan Ackroyd is there. John Landis is there. The music reverberates across the city. It is, by any standards, the perfect PR event.*

Except that nobody is there to witness it. All the crowds, all the fans, all the TV crews, all the paparazzi, are out on the other side of the street where a different drama is playing out. An ancient, banana-yellow, ex-British Telecom van with a giant spliff leaf on the side is surrounded by police. And I mean surrounded. There are cops everywhere and more are arriving by the minute. Sirens are screaming, horns are blaring, traffic is at a complete standstill. In front of the van, a fat bloke in a yellow T-shirt emblazoned with the same spliff leaf is giving interviews to the press while simultaneously trying to avoid arrest. Next to him is another bloke, as thin as the other one is fat, drinking champagne out of a bottle. Together, they look like Laurel and Hardy. A third bloke squats by the van, stripped to the waist, wearing a bandana. Forget the Blues Brothers. Forget Dan Ackroyd. This is the perfect PR event. In one brief moment these three men have managed to cause absolute chaos in the most important street of the most important film festival in the world. Tomorrow, they'll be in every newspaper. They'll be on every TV news show. They'll be the talk of Cannes. They'll be famous.

DISSOLVE TO:

INT. HOTEL BEDROOM. NIGHT. TEN DAYS EARLIER.

An overweight, balding bloke with a pronounced nervous tic sits on the bed.
He is writing on a piece of toilet paper.

SUNDAY, 10 MAY, HOTEL SAINT LOUIS, ST OMER, FRANCE

I've run out of paper, so I'm using this. It's three a.m. Here I
am, in a fleapit of a hotel, in a drab room, on a lumpy
mattress. A hundred flies spin around the single 40-watt
light bulb hanging from the ceiling. A thousand images spin
around in my brain. I am exhausted, exhilarated, numbed,
drained, bewildered and drunk. I always thought Stephen
Loyd was a little mad. I was wrong. He's a lot mad.

To begin at the beginning. Up at six a.m. Leave the
house at seven. Two hours later I meet my team in a café near
Stephen's house. The team is Hannah, Carl (the sound
recordist) and Alan (the Super 8 cameraman). A quick
résumé: Hannah we know. Carl: sweet-tempered, Irish,
funny, charming, drinks pints of Guinness like there's no
tomorrow. Alan: small, moody, hugely talented, never drinks
anything except mineral water. He's brought six Super 8
cameras with him. Some of these are genuinely beautiful
devices, at least twenty years old, lovingly cared for, polished
like gems. Last time I saw Alan his hair was mid-brown.
Now he's dyed it a ghastly nicotine-yellow. He looks

terrible. Apparently, he was processing a roll of film last night and some of the chemicals got mixed up with his hair dye.

Ten minutes later we are outside Stephen's house. Stephen is busy putting the final touches to the cannabis leaf.

Gordon is bashing the van door with a hammer. 'It won't shut,' he says. 'I'm just going to have to hold it all the way to Cannes.'

Spooky's head is under the bonnet. Bits of engine sit on the ground by his feet. 'Carburettor's a fucking mess,' he says. 'We'll be lucky if we get to the fucking Dartford Tunnel let alone the South of fucking France. Hi, I'm Spooky.'

He grins through a row of smashed teeth. He's stripped to the waist, not an ounce of fat on him. A bandanna is wrapped round his head. So this is Spooky. It's the first time I've met him. He's the guy who used to be a nightclub bouncer and now wants to be an actor. He's the guy who's going to put the handcuffs on Harvey Weinstein. He's the guy who's going to jail in Cannes.

'Stephen says you're willing to go to jail in Cannes.'

'Yeah, well,' says Spooky. 'Anything for a laugh.'

To date, Spooky has had two acting roles: a non-speaking part as an eighteenth-century prisoner in a film called *House of Tension* (an inspired piece of casting) and Colin, the seventeen-year-old dopehead, in Stephen's trailer for *Amsterdam*. He hopes to play Colin in the completed movie. 'It's a great part,' he says. 'In my first scene I get to masturbate in front of the camera. The rest of the movie I'm unconscious. I think Steve's a really great writer. Don't you?'

An hour later we're set to go. Stephen and Gordon sit in the front of the van. Spooky sits in the back, along with the three sleeping bags, two tents, 50 tins of baked beans, 80 copies of the script, 2000 stickers, 1400 leaflets and one pair of handcuffs. Belching huge clouds of black smoke, the van pulls out into the street. Gordon holds on to the door. We follow in our Espace. Carl has wired up Stephen and Gordon so we can record their conversation *en route*. Their conversation *en route* consists exclusively of ribald comments on every single passing female. The van is so noisy we can hardly even hear these. I start to panic that my film is quickly turning into a story about a bunch of lager louts on their way to the World Cup. And this is only the beginning of Day One.

Amazingly, we get to Dover. Five minutes into the crossing Stephen, Gordon and Spooky disappear into the bar. Hannah says to me, 'Stephen's just a yob. This story is going down the tubes.'

Carl says, 'Who *are* these guys anyway?'

Alan says, 'Stephen keeps making jokes about my hair.'

I take five seasickness pills and pretend it isn't happening.

By the time we get to Calais it's dark. Stephen stops at a shop called Booze Express and buys six crates of a beer called – of all things – *Amsterdam*. 'It's for publicity purposes,' he says. 'That's if we don't drink the fucking lot first.' Then they proceed to drink the fucking lot first. After ten minutes Stephen starts driving on the wrong side of the road. After twenty minutes he's lost. After two hours he's still ten miles outside Calais.

He flags down a passing motorist. 'Oi, mate, which is the way to Cans?' he yells.

The motorist flees in terror.

An hour later, Stephen flags down another motorist. 'Excuse me, can you tell me the way to Cans?' he says.

'Cans?'

'Cans.'

'Cans?'

'Cans. In the South of France.'

'Ah, vous voulez dire *Cannes*?'

'That's what I said in the first place. Cans.'

'It is very far from here. This is Calais.'

'Is it *still* Calais?'

Then they come to a crossroads.

'Which way, right or left?' says Stephen.

'Left,' says Gordon.

'Are you sure it isn't right?'

'OK, right. Straight over. Left. How the fuck do I know? The map's all in fucking French. Follow the moon.'

'No, follow the North Star,' says Spooky.

'Chuck us another beer, Spooky, there's a good lad,' says Stephen, accelerating towards a set of traffic lights.

CUT TO:

EXT. NIGHT. A COUNTRY ROAD IN NORTHERN FRANCE.

The van screeches round a hairpin bend, swerves across the centre section, skids through a red light and straight towards an oncoming car. We wait for the crash.

CUT TO:

INT. FRONT OF VAN. NIGHT.

Stephen is driving. With one hand he holds an empty beer can. With the other he holds a full beer can. Occasionally, he holds the steering wheel.

STEPHEN

Shit drivers, the Frogs.

GORDON
(*With one hand he also holds a beer can.
With the other he holds the passenger door.*)
What driver? I didn't see any driver.

STEPHEN

Fucking brakes aren't working. You'll have to hold the fucking
handbrake.

GORDON

I can't. I'm holding the door.

CUT TO:

INT. BACK OF VAN. NIGHT.

*Spooky sits on an empty crate of beer, surrounded by empty cans of beer. He
stares into space. Next to him, squeezed between fifty tins of baked beans and a
huge stack of scripts, is Carl. He holds a walkie-talkie and wears a set of
earphones. His face is completely white.*

CUT TO:

INT. CREW VAN. NIGHT.

*We see the other van in front. Alan is filming out of the window. A middle-
aged bald bloke whom we take to be the director keeps popping various coloured
pills into his mouth. This is me.*

138

Over the walkie-talkie we hear Carl.

CARL

Please, God, I don't want to die. Holy Mary Mother of God, don't let me die.

ALAN

I'm awfully glad I'm not Carl right now.

HANNAH

Jesus Christ, they'll kill him! Stop the van! Stephen, you're the fucking director. *Do something!*

(*Beat*)

Stephen? Are you OK?

ME

I feel sick. I think I've taken too many seasickness pills.

CUT TO:

EXT. NIGHT. TWO HOURS LATER. A FRENCH COUNTRY ROAD.

The van pulls over to a lay-by. The back door opens. Spooky gets out, followed by Stephen and Gordon. Carl falls out head first on to the ground. Nobody takes any notice.

'Get the map out, Spook,' Stephen says.
    Spooky gets the map out. They rest it on the bonnet.
    'Right. Here's Calais . . . There's Boulogne . . . So where's Cannes?'
    'There's La Rochelle,' says Spooky.

'There's Bilbao,' Gordon points out.

'Bilbao? Isn't that Spain?' asks Stephen.

'Nah, it's Belgium,' says Spooky.

'It's Italy,' says Gordon. 'All their words end in O.'

'It's definitely Belgium,' says Spooky.

'So where does France stop and Spain begin?' says Stephen.

'I told you we should have followed the moon,' says Gordon.

They all climb back into the van.

Stephen tries to start the engine but nothing happens. He tries again. Still nothing.

'Er . . . we've run out of petrol,' he says.

For a moment, there is complete silence. Then Gordon burps. Then a car passes. Then Stephen says, 'Fucking petrol gauge isn't working.'

Spooky says, 'What are we going to do now?'

CUT TO:

EXT. NIGHT. FRENCH COUNTRY ROAD.

The crew Espace pulls up behind the BT van. Exit Hannah, Alan and me. I film the following exchange with a video camera.

STEPHEN
(*staggers up to me and burps in my face*)
Can you lend us some petrol?

ME
(*fumbling with the video camera*)
Shit, I missed that. Could you just do it again?

140

STEPHEN
(*staggers up to me and burps into my camera*)
Can you lend us some petrol?

ME
No.

STEPHEN
No?

ME
(*looking through the camera*)
No. Don't be silly. We're not here. We don't exist. We're fly on the wall. Just move a couple of inches to your left, will you? It's a better frame.

STEPHEN
Fly on the wall? You're a fly in the fucking ointment.

GORDON
I've just had a totally brilliant idea.

STEPHEN AND SPOOKY
(*together*)
What?

GORDON
Let's have another beer.

A quick calculation. We are 854 miles from Cannes. At this rate Stephen, Gordon and Spooky will reach Cannes on 14 June. That's three weeks after the end of the Film Festival. That's two weeks after the Dentist Convention. That's one week after the end of the Duty Free Convention. That's on the last day of the World Barbie Doll Manufacturers Convention.

My predictions are coming true.

MONDAY, 11 MAY, HOTEL AU MONTCHAPET, DIJON, FRANCE

Breakfast at seven. Then it's back to the spot where we left Stephen, Gordon and Spooky last night. There's no sign of the van. The only evidence there ever was a van is an empty can of beer by the road. Make that three empty cans of beer. Make that eleven. We spend the next half-hour finding assorted bits of debris by the road. The final tally is:

1 car seat (ripped)
1 script of *Amsterdam* (torn)
4 pairs of socks
1 tin of sardines (half-eaten)
1 Iceland plastic bag containing a pile of vomit
1 wheel hub
58 cans of beer (empty)

Where are Stephen, Gordon and Spooky?

Hannah tries Gordon's mobile phone but it's dead. She checks her answering system but there's no message. For several minutes we all stand around, not knowing what to do next. Our story has disappeared. Then Hannah says, 'What if they've been arrested?'

Alan says, 'What if they've crashed?'

Carl says, 'What if they're dead?'

I say, 'Let's call Brian.'

We call Brian. 'Christ,' he says. 'I better call the police.'

'What do we do in the meantime?' I ask.

'How do I know?' says Brian. 'You're the fucking director. Film something.'

I turn to Alan. 'He says film something.'

'Like what?' enquires Alan.

'How the hell do I know?' I reply. 'You're the fucking cameraman.'

Alan starts filming the trees. Then he films the 58 cans of beer on the road. Then he films the tin of sardines. Then he films the trees again. After an hour of this he gets through 12 rolls of film. That's 600 feet. That's £1200. This is the sort of thing Michael Cimino did when he went several times over budget on *Heaven's Gate* and in the process destroyed United Artists.

Then Hannah says, 'I've got an idea. Let's go and have breakfast again.' So we do. We have a long, languid, luxurious breakfast back in the hotel. We have coffee, croissants, eggs, ham, cheese, orange juice. Hell, we're on holiday. There's nothing to do. We've got no story. We've got no characters. Have some more coffee. Have another croissant.

'Let's go swimming this afternoon,' says Alan.

'Let's find a nice restaurant for lunch,' I say.

'Let's go shopping,' says Hannah.

Then the mobile phone rings. It's Brian.

INT. HOTEL RESTAURANT. DAY.

FX phone. The table is covered with the remains of a giant breakfast. The director (me) picks up the phone.

BRIAN

How's the filming going?

143

ME

Terrific.

BRIAN

That's terrific.

(*Beat*)

Well I've phoned the police. There's no sign of them anywhere. I've tried all the hospitals. Nothing. They've simply disappeared.

ME

What about the morgues?

BRIAN

The *morgues?*

ME

In case they're all dead.

BRIAN

Jesus. That's all we fucking need. Did they sign their contracts? Listen. I've got masses to do here. We're flying to Nice tomorrow. I'm up to my ears. Can't you phone the morgues?

ME

Impossible. I'm far too busy filming.

Lunch is at a very pretty restaurant in Soissons. I order the *foie gras;* Hannah the *moules;* Alan the *confit* of duck. We drink two bottles of '83 Pomerol.

We're just about to start on the *tarte tatin* – the house speciality – when the phone rings again.

144

INT. RESTAURANT. DAY.

FX phone. The table is covered with the remains of an enormous lunch. The director (me) picks up the phone.

ME

So, Brian. Are they dead?

GORDON

What?

ME

Jesus. Gordon, is that you?

GORDON

Of course it's me. Where the hell are you?

ME

We're just having lun . . . we're filming.

GORDON

What the fuck happened to you?

ME

What the fuck happened to *you?*

GORDON

It's a long story. I'll tell you when we see you. We're just passing through a town called — wait a sec — Soissons. (*He spells this out.*) I can see a restaurant called — wait a sec — the Pot d'Etain. (*He spells this out too.*) It's got green shutters. Meet us there as soon as you've finished your filming.

POV from restaurant window where the crew are sitting. A bright-yellow van with a cannabis leaf on the side pulls up outside.

✳

'We've lost Spooky,' says Stephen.

'You've *what?*'

'Spooky. He's gone. We've lost him.'

'Some documentary crew you lot are,' says Gordon. 'You fucking missed *everything.*'

And this is what we missed.

After we left them last night, Gordon hitched a lift to the nearest petrol station, filled up a can of petrol, hitched a lift back to the van. Despite the fact that Stephen was several times over the limit, he decided to make for Dijon. Then Gordon, in a sudden fit of temper, chucked the only road map they had out of the window. Then Stephen kicked Gordon in the balls. Then Gordon punched Stephen in the jaw. As a result, Stephen's face has swollen up like a balloon. All this did not augur well for their relationship as producer and director. More to the point, they still had another 386 miles to go to Dijon.

By this time Stephen's blood was up. He insisted on driving very fast on small country lanes. Without brakes. Over the limit. On the wrong side of the road. What happened next is a bit of a mystery but Stephen reckons it must have been the hairpin bend with the 400-foot drop on the side towards which he was accelerating at 90 miles an hour that made Spooky decide he'd finally had enough. But he's not sure. What we do know — now — is that at some point Spooky jumped out of the back of the van, ran down the side of a hill, tripped over a fence and fell face first into a ditch.

Meanwhile, Stephen and Gordon were too busy arguing to notice, and drove on through the night, leaving Spooky in his ditch. This might have been merely amusing, except that Spooky not only had managed to knock himself unconscious, he'd also taken all the money with him.

146

DISSOLVE TO:

FLASHBACK. INT. VAN. NIGHT. THREE HOURS AFTER SPOOKY
HAS BASHED HIS HEAD IN A DITCH

STEPHEN
Here, Spooky, chuck us another beer, will you?

(*Beat*)

Spooky?

Stephen and Gordon look behind them. The back door of the van is wide open.

GORDON
Fuck me. He's gone.

The van screeches to a sudden halt.

'That's when the police turned up with their sniffer dogs,'
says Gordon.
'*Sniffer dogs?*' I ask.
'Yeah,' says Gordon. 'They wanted to check out the van.'
'They thought we had drugs,' adds Stephen.
'Which, of course, we didn't,' says Gordon.
'So we told them we were going to the Cannes Film
Festival.'
'And we gave them a copy of the script,' says Gordon.
'And some stickers.'
'And a leaflet.'
'And Gordon did his pitch.'
'The two-minute version.'
'Which they *loved*.'

147

'And then they left.'

I ask, 'You're saying all this happened in *one night*?'

'Yeah,' says Stephen. 'And you fucking missed the lot.'

Apparently, Spooky phoned early this morning. Now he's taking the train to Cannes. ('His 'ead's a bit bashed about,' says Stephen, 'but otherwise he's OK.') Meanwhile, Stephen and Gordon have got exactly £8.46 (78 francs) between them. And 486 miles to go. And no map.

'How do you find your way without a map?' I ask.

'Well,' says Gordon, 'in the morning we just kept the sun on our left.'

'And in the afternoon,' adds Stephen, 'we'll just keep it on our right.'

'Or is it the other way round?' asks Gordon.

Jesus. All this in *twelve hours*? This is Oscar-winning stuff. Things happen to these guys. And this is only Day Two. What will it be like in Cannes (assuming they ever get there)? I have just two fears: (a) that everybody will think Stephen and Gordon are actors, that we've set the whole thing up, start to finish. False – but very credible under the circumstances. I'd believe it if I were watching. Then there's (b). (b) is I keep missing the story. Last night was a lesson. In future, I resolve to stick to Stephen and Gordon like glue. To stay up all hours. To keep them always in my sights. To be their shadow. To miss – *nothing*.

TUESDAY, 12 MAY,
EN ROUTE TO CANNES

Last night, while I was fast asleep in bed, Stephen and Gordon nearly got arrested.

They came at dawn. Sniffer dogs again, two car-loads of cops, guns, customs police, the works. The van was parked off the main Dijon–Beaune road in a vineyard. We'd left them at three a.m. This time, the police really meant business. They turned the van over. They checked under the seats. They stuck a mirror under the chassis. They looked in the engine. They opened the baked beans. Stephen offered them stickers. Gordon tried the pitch. But this lot weren't buying it. And the reason? Apparently, in France, it's illegal even to *depict* a cannabis leaf – let alone smoke one. If tried and convicted, they face a fine of 500,000 francs. Or they get deported. Or they go to jail.

The implications for Stephen and Gordon are disastrous. First there's the van. Two cannabis leaves there. Then 80 copies of the script (cannabis leaf on the cover). Then 1400 leaflets (cannabis leaf on the cover of that). Then 75 T-shirts (big cannabis leaf on the front). Then 2000 stickers (all cannabis leaf). *Everything* has a cannabis leaf on it. Their whole publicity campaign is based on the fact. For days and nights, Stephen drove his minicab all over London for one purpose: to pay people to print cannabis leaves on every single bit of publicity material he's got. So now what?

'Big kickings coming in Cannes,' says Stephen. 'That's what.'

10.15 a.m. We are 40 miles outside Dijon. It is 318 miles to Cannes. Stephen and Gordon stop at a service station to buy breakfast. Since they've now got exactly £5.57 between them, they have to share a shower (£3). Breakfast is a stale baguette (30p) filled with cold baked beans. That leaves £2.27 for petrol.

10.17 a.m. Hannah buys breakfast for Alan, Carl and me.

Coffee, tea, eggs, smoked ham, *chèvre* cheese, *paté aux truffes*, hot rolls, toast, little pats of Isigny butter, salami, three different kinds of jam, marmalade, freshly squeezed mango juice, four bars of Swiss chocolate. We sit in the sun to eat. Stephen asks if he can have some. I tell him not to be silly.

10.34 a.m. Stephen reckons the van will do 30 miles to the gallon. The tank is three-quarters full. This means he'll probably run out of petrol ten miles outside Cannes. He spends half an hour tinkering with the carburettor to lower the consumption while we start on our ice-creams.

10.39 a.m. Gordon reads the *Amsterdam* leaflet to camera. It says:

Are you looking for that single distribution territory to add to your existing feature film library?

Feel capable of taking on world-wide rights excluding UK from the UK's newest independent distributor?

If the answer to either of those questions is yes, Stephen Loyd says:
COME AND HAVE A GO IF YOU THINK YOU'RE HARD ENOUGH!

'We put our phone number at the bottom,' says Gordon, 'but unfortunately it's the wrong number.'
   'It's the wrong number?'
   'We forgot to put a 4 in it.'
   'Exactly how many leaflets have you printed?'
   'One thousand four hundred and thirty-seven,' says Gordon.

*

11.45 a.m. 300 miles to go. The sun is high in the sky. Temperature 80F and climbing. I stick my hand out of the window and feel the warm breeze. The landscape is changing. Vineyards shimmer in the midday heat. Dramatic outcrops of rocks. Tiny villages perched on the tops of hills. Stalls selling oranges on the side of the road. A few moments ago we passed our first palm tree. The South beckons. Everybody is getting excited.

2.30 p.m. 180 miles to Cannes. Stephen has just decided that the quickest way there is to take the autoroute.

2.46 p.m. Stephen jumps the autoroute toll barrier.

2.48 p.m. Stephen is stopped by the police.

2.51 p.m. A second police van turns up, this time with six sniffer dogs. Stephen gives each policeman a sticker, a leaflet and a copy of the script. The police respond by setting the sniffer dogs on the van.

3.02 p.m. The police don't find any drugs. But they love the script.

4.16 p.m. 92 miles to Cannes. Stephen and Gordon discuss the film. Gordon says, 'I can see it in my head and Steve can see it in his head but what we need to do is compare heads, if you see what I mean?'

4.22 p.m. Stephen and Gordon have an amicable discussion about the pitch.

4.23 p.m. Stephen and Gordon come to blows over the pitch.

Stephen says Gordon hasn't captured the essence of the story. Gordon says it's difficult to capture the essence of the story when (a) you've only got 30 seconds and (b) your nose is bleeding.

4.24 p.m. Stephen begins his version of the pitch.

4.35 p.m. Stephen pitching.

4.46 p.m. Stephen still pitching.

4.59 p.m. Stephen still pitching.

5.04 p.m. Stephen still pitching. Gordon is asleep.

5.16 p.m. Stephen still pitching. Carl runs out of tape.

5.21 p.m. Stephen ends pitch. Gordon wakes up.

5.36 p.m. 27 miles to Cannes. Less than a quarter of a tank of petrol left.

5.57 p.m., 14 miles. Dusk. First sight of the sea. A thousand lights twinkling in the bay. Stephen very excited. Me too. The needle is on the red.

6.24 p.m. 6 miles. In the suburbs. Stephen pulls up at a road sign. It says 'Cannes Est' and 'Cannes Ouest'. Gordon gets out his phrase-book. He says, 'Ouest is East and Est is West. Or is it the other way round?'

6.37 p.m. A huge neon sign stretched across the road. It says: BIENVENU AU FILM FESTIVAL DE CANNES. A million light bulbs draped in the trees. The streets jammed with traffic, the cafés and restaurants packed. Makeshift barriers in the road. The thud of music from a hundred bars. Film posters on every hoarding, every building, every wall. *Armageddon. Godzilla.* Bruce Willis. Hugh Grant. A news crew on a street corner. Another opposite just setting up a camera. A white stretch limo parked by a cinema. Crowds of fans outside the Carlton Hotel. Fountains playing. A bunch of paparazzi. The marina with a million yachts. A couple on the quay, wearing evening dress, holding hands. The Palais, with its huge illuminated blue sign: 51ÈME FESTIVAL DE FILM DE CANNES 1998. A sudden glimpse of red-carpeted steps. The long stretch of the Croisette, flanked by palm trees gently swaying in the evening sea breeze. The moon, unnaturally large, hanging over the bay. A bloke in a yellow T-shirt with a cannabis leaf, and a big piece of Elastoplast stuck on his nose.

'*Spooooky!*' yells Stephen. And, as he does so, the van runs out of petrol.

Cannes. At last.

WEDNESDAY, 13 MAY, CANNES

OK. So here we all are, together again, one big happy family. Brian. Pascale. Dave, my cameraman. His assistant, Mike. A second Irish sound recordist. Several production assistants. Bronwen. Another, all-Irish, crew joins us at the weekend. The production has its base in a flat near the town centre. This morning, a table is set for breakfast on the balcony. The sun rises over the hills. A church bell rings. Nothing stirs, despite the fact it's nine thirty in the morning. Today is the first day of the Festival and every producer, distributor,

153

agent, exhibitor, actor, director and journalist in town is fast asleep in bed.

But not us. We have things to discuss. Strategies. Tactics. Schedules. Rosters. Brian gets out his fabulously complicated multi-coloured circuit diagram and says, 'Well, I'm glad Stephen and Gordon weren't killed in a car crash. Otherwise I'd have to do this schedule all over again.'

Frank and Aaron arrive tomorrow. The helicopter is all set up. James Merendino arrives on Friday, Mike Hakata on Saturday. Today is therefore an easy day: just the *Amsterdam* team and Erick Zonca. He flies in this afternoon. Over breakfast we decide to split forces. I'll link up with Stephen, and Pascale will meet Zonca at Nice airport. A nice, simple, straightforward day. What could possibly go wrong?

CUT TO:

EXT. CROISETTE. DAY.

The van is parked in the middle of the street. Surrounding it are about a hundred teenage kids, all yelling at the tops of their voices. Some are trying to stick 100-franc notes through the window. Others are banging on the side of the van.

STEPHEN
(*he shouts over the noise of the crowds*)
Fuck off! Go away! I already told you! We're not selling any drugs! We're selling a fucking *movie!*

SPOOKY
Give 'em a leaflet, Steve.

GORDON

Give 'em a sticker, Steve.

STEPHEN

Oh, shit. It's the cops.

A policeman elbows his way through the crowd.

As part of his campaign to raise £1.2 million, Stephen spends most of the morning driving up and down the Croisette blasting the horn. I suspect this is because he doesn't know what else to do. Maybe he just feels safe in the driving seat. If so, I don't blame him. There is something indefinably intimidating about this place. And I've only been here a few hours. Whether it's the overt display of success, the sense of exclusion from a club in which everybody seems to know everybody else, the crass – but somehow affecting – division between the haves and have-nots, the sheer concentration of power and wealth and glamour in one tiny area of one small seaside town . . . I don't know. Back in England, Stephen said to me, 'I don't give a fuck who these people are. If I end up making movies, then that's the industry I'll be in. If I end up pissing everybody off, then I'm still a minicab driver.' It sounded great in Leytonstone. But out here, well – it's a different ball game.

As for Gordon, he simply pitches the story to *everyone*. He pitches it (in all four versions) to tourists, to waiters, to doormen, to people stuck in traffic, to others lying on the beach, to street sweepers, to hot-dog salesmen, to window cleaners, to ice-cream vendors, to the man putting up the poster for *Notting Hill* opposite the Martinez Hotel, to chauffeurs lounging beside their limos, to the human statue by the Majestic pier, to six-year-old kids riding the carousel on the sea front, to their mums and dads, to an old tramp sitting on a park bench, to a bunch of Australian backpackers, to an ancient prostitute in a leopard-skin miniskirt opposite the Petit Carlton bar, to my crew, to me – to everyone, that is, except the people who really matter.

After a couple of hours of this Gordon gets bored. So he starts stickering women's bottoms instead. Then he starts stickering policemen when they're not looking. By midday, half the police force in Cannes are walking around town with a picture of a cannabis leaf stuck on their back. Well, almost.

After lunch, Stephen and Gordon slip past the barrier into the Carlton Hotel to nick some toiletries. They take the lift to the fourth floor. While Gordon distracts the chambermaid by giving her the sixty-second version of the pitch (in French), Stephen nicks several bars of soap, towels, hand cream, shaving utensils, shampoo. They also put a sticker on every door. Then Stephen says, 'Well, I think that's enough for one day. Let's go and get pissed.'

The British Pavilion is one of the best places to get pissed in Cannes, chiefly because the drinks are free. (Lots of things are free here. For instance, I've discovered you can get a free pair of Ray-Bans every time you do an interview in the American Pavilion.) The British Pavilion is the same as all the others: huge tents which sprawl along the length of the Croisette. When I came last month, none of them existed. In a couple of weeks they'll all be gone. But today they dominate the sea front, like the sails of great ships, every one packed with people drinking, shmoozing, networking, doing deals. Stephen, Gordon and Spooky sit down at a table. They look curiously out of place. Nobody is doing deals with them.

'What we've got to do,' says Stephen, 'is a bit of snurging.'

Snurging?

'Yeah, you know. Bang a few heads. Make people sit up.'

'Create a bit of excitement.'

'Use the handcuffs.'

'Maybe let the tyres down on the Croisette.'

'Set fire to the van.'

'Anything to make people realise we're serious film-makers.'

Back at the office I find Pascale, flushed with excitement about Erick Zonca. She and Alan went to film his arrival at the airport this morning. At first he was completely ignored. Then Alan started filming him. Instantly he was surrounded. Fans started begging for his autograph. Photographers snapped their cameras at him. News crews rushed to join the throng. Suddenly, every reporter in the building was thrusting a microphone in his face. Nobody had the remotest clue who he was. They were just scared shitless of missing the story.

CUT TO:

INT. DAY. AIRPORT ARRIVALS LOUNGE.

Erick Zonca stands in the middle of a crowd of reporters.

REPORTER NO. I

So are you very excited to be in Cannes?

ZONCA

Well, I –

157

REPORTER NO. 2
This is a great moment for you. A milestone in your career. Can you describe for our viewers what's going through your head right now?

ZONCA
Well, you see, I —

REPORTER NO. 3
Are you feeling nervous? Apprehensive? Excited?

ZONCA
Well, you see, I've only just arr —

REPORTER NO. 2
OK. Cut. That was great. Fantastic. Thanks. By the way, I just have to say I thought you were terrific in your last movie.

ZONCA
My last movie? This is my first movie.

REPORTER NO. 2
Exactly. Your first movie. What a performance. What charisma. What style. Who was the director again?

ZONCA
Me.

This, then, is Cannes: 5000 journalists chasing a limited number of stories, every day, every night, for two weeks. Everybody filming everybody else. Everybody filming everybody filming everybody else. Everybody filming everybody filming everybody . . . And so it goes on. One big crazy game of Blind Man's Buff.

✳

A piece of bad news this evening. The Cannes Festival Office has turned down our request to suspend a camera from the roof of the Palais steps on Sunday. Sunday is Zonca's Big Night, the moment when his movie will be screened for the very first time before an audience of 2400 people. Like everyone else with a movie in Competition, Zonca will walk up the red carpet to the accompaniment of hundreds of TV cameras and thousands of fans (99.9 per cent of whom won't have a clue who he is). The music from his movie will be broadcast from loudspeakers. His producer, his co-writer, his actors and actresses, will walk up the steps with him. Police in ceremonial uniform will stand to attention as he passes. A thousand flashbulbs will burst in his face. It is, by any standards, an orgy of celebration (enough to swell the tiniest, most shrivelled ego to monster-sized proportions, enough to swell mine). Hence the request to suspend the camera from the roof. It would make a fantastic shot. Brian says the reason it's been refused is because the Festival Office are terrified the camera will fall down and hit Erick Zonca on the head — thereby killing him at the moment of his greatest triumph.

THURSDAY, 14 MAY, CANNES

This morning Frank and Aaron are arriving in Cannes by helicopter. Let me start that sentence again. This morning Frank and Aaron won't arrive in Cannes by helicopter because in fact they arrived yesterday by bus. But I'm the only one who knows it (apart from them of course). As far as my audience is concerned, they arrived by helicopter. Today. Who said anything about a bus? Hence my plan: to pick them up from their Cannes hotel, drive them 40 miles to

Nice airport, stick them on a helicopter and fly them 40 miles all the way back to Cannes again. As if they've just arrived. This is what is meant by the miracle of film. All they need is a couple of empty suitcases.

Potentially, this is a dangerous thing to do. It steps perilously close to the blurred edges of the Deliberate Lie. And as we all know, documentaries never lie. So why am I doing it? One reason is a fetish for symmetry. I have four characters. Zonca arrives by plane, takes a chauffeur-driven car to Cannes. Mike arrives by plane, takes the bus. James Merendino arrives by train (from Italy), takes a taxi from the station. Stephen and Gordon arrive by . . . well, we know how *they* arrive. That leaves Frank and Aaron. Young, hotshot producers, in Cannes to raise £20m, armed with a slate of six projects. How do they arrive? By bus. How *should* they arrive? By helicopter.

It's wrong and I know it's wrong. The trouble is the helicopter is already booked. It's costing us a thousand quid. If we dump it now, we lose all the money (I lose my testicles). I've made a bad decision, a rushed decision, but I'm committed to it. I live – or fall – by the consequences. It doesn't help that Frank and Aaron aren't happy either.

'Why are we doing this?' they ask in the taxi on the way to Nice.

'It's the symmetry,' I say mysteriously.

'What symmetry?'

'The symmetry symmetry. Plus it's all paid for. Plus you're supposed to be hotshot producers. Hotshot producers don't arrive by *bus*, for Chrissake. Also you get a great view.'

And you do. The view is magnificent. Forget the bus. (What bus?) We sweep like gods over the coast, over the bays and inlets fringed by snow-white beaches, over villages, towns, high-rise hotels and apartment blocks, over luxurious villas, exotic swimming pools and fabulous castles, the whole vista framed by a backdrop of mountains plunging down to the sea. I'm in the front. Frank and Aaron are in the back with Dave, my cameraman. They're saying something about £20m but I'm not listening . . . because we've just cleared a ridge, climbed over a hill, banked round a promontory and there, suddenly emerging through the haze, is . . . Cannes.

From up here it looks like fantasy town, a fairy city of pavilions, towers, palm trees bleached by light. For the first time, since beginning this film, I see the place for what it represents, not for what it is. Down there, I know, is reality. A tough, back-breaking, heartless struggle to make a name, to sit on top of the hill. But from where I'm sitting right now it's a palace of dreams, beautiful, seductive, untouchable in the morning sun. Even Frank and Aaron stop talking. We all stare out of the windows. The helicopter swoops towards the city. In a couple of minutes it is all over.

'That was truly wonderful,' says Aaron. And so it was.

Then the phone rings. It's Brian.

'Get the hell over to the Martinez Hotel,' he says. 'Zonca's waiting. He's pissed off. Alan and Pascale are already there.'

Reality.

The Martinez is one of the three grand hotels which line the sea front. (The other two are the Majestic and the Carlton.) We walk into the lobby to find Pascale and Alan. Both of them are wearing new pairs of Ray-Bans.

Pascale fills me in. The reason why Zonca is pissed off is because an article in a French newspaper has been making fun of him. Apparently, he turned up to some formal event in a dinner suit but forgot to take his trainers off. As a result he is extremely suspicious of us. He's turned down our request for an interview. Instead, he says, we can interview him being interviewed by somebody else. This is a dangerous precedent, not least because the somebody else in question is a French journalist who asks astonishingly anodyne questions in the style of a BBC reporter *circa* 1953 interviewing the Prime Minister. I want to ask Zonca whether he's terrified out of his wits at the prospect of 2400 people watching his movie on Sunday. I want to ask him why he forgot to take his trainers off. But all we get is:

'Would it be too much trouble to ask you to specify the various cinematic influences in your work?'

or:

'*La Vie Revée des Anges* is a most interesting title. I'd be very grateful if you could explain why you chose it.'

or:

'Have you met the famous Greek director Angelopoulos yet?'

All I can do is film it. Zonca, to his credit, looks bored out of his brain. We all are (except Pascale, who – being a cinephile – seems to find this sort of thing quite interesting). The only highlight of the whole interview is when Stephen and Gordon's British Telecom van comes tootling along the Croisette outside the hotel, blasting the 'Charge of the Cavalry' at full volume. Everybody looks up, startled. I begin to giggle. It's as if some drunken lout had suddenly burst in on a rather polite dinner party. No doubt Pascale would say it was pure Buñuel. So would I if I'd seen any of his movies.

After the interview, Zonca disappears.

My cameraman says, 'Well wasn't that just the most interesting interview you ever heard in your life?'

Pascale says, 'Isn't Erick wonderful? I loved the bit when he talked about Angelopoulos. So fascinating. So . . . *insightful*.'

I say this story is shit.

'Shit?' she asks.

'Shit,' I reply. 'The only good bit was when Stephen Loyd went past in the van, blasting his horn.'

'Oh, *that*,' says Pascale. 'Pure Buñuel, I thought.'

More Zonca in the afternoon, this time on the roof terrace of the Martinez Hotel where he's about to be fitted up with a dinner suit for his Big Night. Like the Oscars, every nominee is fitted up with complimentary dinner suits/gowns/jewellery/underwear by Big Name Designers for their Big Night. Predictably, Pascale knows the names of all the Big Name Designers. She's clearly shocked that I don't. And that I don't care. Interestingly, I'm one with Zonca on this. He's clearly not at all happy about the whole process of transforming himself from France's answer to Ken Loach into a mannequin.

The roof terrace is another world, stuffed with the rich, the beautiful and the famous. This is my first insight into a very different side of Cannes. We're a long way from Stephen's van and the attentions of the police. Up here, the police don't bust you for drugs. Up here they guard you, escort you, defer to you, protect you from the hideous masses. (After all, this is Cannes and even the cops know their Jean Renoir from their Jean Vigo.) Everybody drinks bucket-loads of champagne, including Zonca who's already had ten glasses by the time we get to him and is a touch unsteady on his feet. With him is his co-writer Virginie, a cool blonde with cool eyes whose English is clearly better than she pretends and who, I have decided, has taken an instant dislike to me. At one point, Claudia Schiffer (an even cooler blonde) gets in the way of the camera and I have to ask her to move. She looks utterly bewildered. This is probably the very first time in her life that anybody with a camera has ever asked her to get *out* of the shot. But she does.

Zonca disappears downstairs for his fitting while we wait. I feel slightly fraudulent in this little oasis of privilege and spend a lot of time pretending to eat peanuts. After fifteen minutes, I go down to find Zonca all dressed up and standing by the lift. A quick glance at his feet. No trainers. It transpires the complimentary dinner suit is getting a trial run. He and Virginie are off to a friend's screening at the Palais. I ask if I can go too. Before he has a chance to say no, I jump in the lift. For the next four floors I have him all to myself. This is my chance. No more crap about Angelopoulos or the title of his film. What I want to know is what everybody wants to know. How does it *feel*?

'It feels tight,' he says.

'Tight?'

'Tight, yes.'

He means his bow tie, for Chrissake.

'Also, I haven't shaved.'

'You haven't shaved.'

'No.'

The doors slide open. *Shit.* That's four whole floors' worth of interview chucked away. I could kick myself. I pursue Zonca into the lobby, all marble and chandeliers and gorgeous women and a million paparazzi. Despite the fact that it's three o'clock in the afternoon, everybody, including the paparazzi, is in evening dress. Now I'm the only one wearing trainers. Zonca goes out to his car. I ask if I can go too. Before he has a chance to say no, I jump in. The car starts to move through crowds of tourists, fans, celebrity spotters, photographers, reporters, news cameramen. A battery of lights flash in the windscreen. Someone bangs on the door. Someone else sticks his tongue out at my camera. Behind us, a cheer goes up. It's Claudia Schiffer emerging from the lobby. This time nobody asks her to get out of the way. For a brief moment, I experience the dizzying aura of fame. Suddenly I too am one of the privileged. So this is what it feels like. To be on the inside. To be celebrated. To be blessed. Me and Erick and Claudia together. We're all in the same boat. For a few startling, confusing, exhilarating seconds, we're all Kings of Cannes.

Almost before it started it's over. Now it's back to business. From the Martinez to the Palais is half a mile. That's about five minutes. With these crowds, maybe ten at the most. Ten minutes to win this guy over, ten minutes to build a relationship based on trust, understanding and mutual respect. Ten minutes to see if there's even a story. I haven't got time to waste. While Erick is still dealing with the fact I'm even in his car, I flick the camera switch to ON.

INT. ZONCA'S LIMO. DAY.

Zonca and Virginie are in the back. I'm in the front. The camera points at Zonca's head like a gun.

ME: Erick, you can't move without people interviewing you, photographing you, filming you. Do you hate it?

ZONCA: Yes.

ME: Have you ever experienced anything like this before?

ZONCA: No.

Me: Did you expect this sort of reaction before you got here?

165

ZONCA: No.

ME: Have you ever been to Cannes before?

ZONCA: Yes.

ME: Are you excited about your big screening on Sunday?

ZONCA: Yes.

ME: Are you nervous?

ZONCA: No.

Having completely run out of things to ask, we all sit in total silence for the next five minutes.

ME: Are you fed up with people asking you silly questions?

At this point Erick starts to laugh. So do I. The ice is definitely broken.

'The ice is definitely broken,' I say to Pascale afterwards. 'If I'm any judge of character, I'd say he really likes me.'

'Oh, yes?' she says. 'Well, I've got news for you. Erick called me half an hour ago. He fucking hates you. And he's pulling out of the film.'

'He's *what*?'

'Boy, you really fucked things up this time.'

FRIDAY, 15 MAY, CANNES

OK, time to regroup. I'm in the doghouse. With Zonca out, we've lost a key element in the story. We've lost the Competition, we've lost the glamour, we've lost the razzmatazz. None of our other characters provides this. To

166

give the film tension, we need contrast. Stephen Loyd at one extreme, Erick Zonca at the other. The others in the middle. Take Zonca out of the picture and the whole structure collapses like a pack of cards. To put it another way, Zonca is the yardstick by which all the others measure their achievement. He's at the top of the tree. They're still climbing it.

Let's get one thing straight. I never expected to be intimate with Zonca. I never expected him to hand us the key to his soul, to his innermost fears, hopes, doubts, ambitions. There obviously wasn't time to build that sort of relationship (even if he'd liked me). Certainly, it would have been a bonus. But it was never the crux. The crux was what he represented. And what he represented was everything all our other characters dream about every day of their lives. What he represented was success.

And now he's gone. Pascale is still seething with anger. I feel sick. I spent half the night staring at the walls, smoking a hundred fags, wondering what went wrong. I've been in Cannes sixty hours and I'm already exhausted. And we've still got Mike Hakata and James Merendino to come. How am I going to cope? The weekend looms ahead like some horrible catastrophe, pre-sealed, pre-packaged, pre-ordained. With my name on it.

After breakfast we gather for a crisis meeting. The first question is this: who replaces Zonca? Of course, we've still got Frank and Aaron. Hannah spent yesterday afternoon following them around. She's not optimistic. Their story is descending into an endless series of business meetings. Great for them, dull for us. She shows me bits of her video. It looks like . . . an endless series of business meetings. Five minutes of that and 99.9 per cent of the audience will be watching the snooker. So what else have we got? Brian gets out the Festival brochure. We scan the list of names in Competition. Perhaps we can replace Zonca with some-body in the same boat? There's Ken Loach. Too famous. There's Theo Angelopoulos. Too serious. There's John Boorman. Too famous again. There's Roberto Benigni. Roberto Benigni? Now *there's* a possibility. He's a sort of Italian version of Woody Allen who's directed a film called *La Vita è Bella* (*Life Is Beautiful*). Set in the Second World War, it's the story of a Jewish father who protects his son by pretending the Holocaust is some sort of giant joke, a fantastic game designed exclusively for their benefit. Ap-parently, it's tipped to win the *Palme d'Or*. Benigni himself is supposed to be hugely eccentric. All of which sounds promising, except . . . it's not his first film. Even if we got him, we lose the point of our story. Sure, we get the glamour, the red carpet, the access to privilege. But our film is supposed to be about first-timers. Benigni isn't a first-timer. Include him and we end up with just another film about Cannes.

The whole meeting rapidly descends into a version of the Mad Hatter's Tea Party. Here we are, three days into the Festival, five months into research, £150,000 already blown on equipment, personnel, resources . . . and we're still try-ing to find a character. How did we let this happen? More to the point, how did *I* let this happen? The morning dis-appears as Brian, Pascale and I smoke our way through three packets of Marlboro Lights and try to work it out. Finally we come up with a decision. Which is to say we don't come up with a decision. Which is to say Pascale will use all her wiles to get Zonca back in the film. And I . . . I will just keep away.

Now we split forces. Pascale to Zonca. Hannah to Frank

and Aaron for one last chance. Me to Stephen & Co. I meet my crew outside by the van. All of them, I notice, are wearing brand-new Ray-Bans.

We whizz out to the camp site. The camp site is where Stephen, Gordon and Spooky are now staying, along with loads of other desperate, starving, impecunious would-be film-makers hoping to make a splash in Cannes. Out here, in the suburbs of the city, there's a whole subculture of obsessives, a sort of underground community of wannabes and has-beens and might-once-have-beens, all living together in unholy proximity. It's an exact mirror image of the Hotel du Cap, in which everything is back to front, upside-down, inside out . . . and lots more fun. This is one reason why the *Amsterdam* team pitched camp here. The other reason is that Gordon and Spooky were fed up with the smell of Stephen's feet. Now they have their own tents.

To date, they are no closer to their £1.2 million. The van has been attracting lots of attention but all of this is (a) from the police and (b) from teenage kids who think they're selling drugs and not a movie. Clearly (a) is contingent upon (b), which is why Stephen and Gordon spend a large part of their days (and nights) being stopped, pulled over, searched, raided and generally sniffed at by various dogs.

CUT TO:

EXT. CAMP SITE. DAY.

Stephen slaps half a bottle of Factor 15 on his nose. He wears a dressing-gown with the logo of the Martinez Hotel. Gordon washes his hair. The shampoo bottle says Compliments Of The Carlton Hotel. We Hope You Have a Pleasant Stay.

ME: So how many times have you been stopped by the
police?

GORDON: Five.

STEPHEN: Six.

GORDON: Five.

STEPHEN: Six.

GORDON: Five.

STEPHEN: Six.

GORDON: No, once on the first night, once on the second
night, once on the autoroute when we crashed the barrier and
twice yesterday when they came with the dogs again.

STEPHEN: Is it five? It just feels like six.

 (*Beat*)

GORDON: If we were selling the movie to the fucking police
we'd be millionaires by now.

(*He squirts eau-de-Cologne on his face from a bottle which says Compliments
Of The Majestic Hotel For The Use Of Our Guests Only.*)

Fifteen minutes later, with Gordon smelling like a tart's
window-box, we pile into the van and drive into town.
    'Today', says Stephen, 'I'm feeling lucky.'
    And he blasts the 'Charge of the Cavalry' all the way into
Cannes.
    They've changed their tactics. Two days ago it was all
pitch pitch pitch to every backpacker in town. Now Stephen
and Gordon are more discriminating. Now they hang around

the Bunker waiting to buttonhole any adult human who looks remotely like he's got £1.2 million to blow. This includes anyone in a suit, anyone with an American accent, anyone with a security escort, anyone getting in or out of a stretch limo, anyone with a big sign saying MY NAME IS HARVEY WEINSTEIN round his neck. Despite the fact that Gordon has spent the last five days practising all three versions of the pitch, it's Stephen who does all the talking all the time. And I mean *all* the time. Not even the people he's talking to get the chance to talk back. Unless it's to say no.

The interesting thing is that nobody says no. There are complex psychological reasons for this (e.g. Stephen is a big guy and his breath reeks of alcohol). The fact is, nobody who knows anything about the movie business says no to anything. Ever. They also don't say yes. They say maybe. Perhaps. Sounds terrific. We'll see. Call my secretary. Here's my business card. Let's do breakfast. Let's do lunch. They say nothing that commits them and nothing that doesn't commit them. Commitment is dangerous. Commitment means either you lose money or the competition makes money. Commitment means answering to your boss.

The trouble is that Stephen doesn't see this. Within thirty minutes he thinks he's made his £1.2 million ten times over. He's all ready to set fire to the van and collect the insurance. 'Didn't I say I was feeling lucky?' he asks. 'You did,' answers Gordon. 'But you aren't.' Gordon is no fool. As a film editor, he's been in the business a little longer than Stephen (who's been in it five days). What Gordon sees is a big fat bloke in a yellow T-shirt exhaling beer fumes all over clean-cut producers who've just had lunch at the Martinez Hotel. And he's angry. In fact, he's more than angry. He's absolutely furious.

CUT TO:

INT. VAN. DAY.

Stephen and Gordon are yelling at each other in the front. We are in the back, squeezed between various bags of dirty underwear, several complimentary toiletry packs (courtesy of the Grand Hotel) and Spooky.

GORDON: If we meet people who might be useful, there's no need to fuck them off.

STEPHEN: I'm not fucking them off. Who am I fucking off?

GORDON: Everybody.

STEPHEN: Everybody?

GORDON: We've got a golden opportunity here, Steve.

STEPHEN: Who have I fucked off?

GORDON: This is a small town.

STEPHEN: Who have I fucked off?

GORDON: Everybody knows us already.

STEPHEN: Who have I fucked off?

GORDON: You can't just go around intimidating people.

STEPHEN: *Intimidating people?*

GORDON: Yeah, you're intimidating. One, you're fat. Two, you're loud. Three, you talk too much.

Afterwards, Gordon says to me, 'The trouble with Steve is he thinks he's still driving a fucking cab in fucking Leytonstone.'

I have never seen Gordon so angry. They've been in Cannes three days and the whole relationship is falling apart.

Stephen spends the rest of the evening sulking up at the camp site. I try to get an interview with him, but he refuses. 'Get out of my fucking hair,' he says. So we do. The crew is silent on the way back to town. It isn't hard to read their thoughts. We've lost Zonca. We're about to dump Frank and Aaron. And now this. One by one our stories are biting the dust. Where will it all end?

Back at the production office, Brian tries to cheer me up by showing off his new Ray-Bans. It doesn't help.

SATURDAY, 16 MAY, CANNES

Off to Nice airport again, to meet Mike Hakata and his producer Rolf. No helicopter this time. We're going by bus. Mike greets us at the terminal building. He carries his six red cans of film and he's in fantastic spirits. He's also exhausted. 'I'm living on black coffee and roll-ups,' he says. 'I haven't slept for four days.' I haven't slept for four days either, except I'm not in fantastic spirits. But Mike helps to cheer me up. His optimism is boundless. 'Everybody wants to know about *Mice*,' he says. 'Even on the plane. I had terrific conversations with the stewardess.'

'Is she going to buy the movie?'

'Listen,' says Mike. 'We're going to sell this fucker.' He slaps one of the film cans. 'In fact,' he adds, 'I'm hoping we're going to sell it today. That way I get six whole days on the beach.' He looks out of the window. The sea glints in the morning light. Cafés, restaurants, shops, posters, palm trees flash by. We shoot under a bridge. Then through a tunnel. The bus moves into the fast lane. A sign: CANNES 8 KMS. Up in the sky, a helicopter banks steeply over the bay. If only. Mike grins at me. 'So this is it,' he says. 'I've got my film cans, I've got my fags, the sun is shining and I'm ready to GO.'

And I feel it too, this exhilaration of the moment. Mike's enthusiasm is infectious. No wonder people work with him for nothing. I'd work with him for nothing. I feel suddenly excited, determined, full of energy. Screw the problems. Screw Zonca. Screw Cannes. Everything is going to be just fine.

Then the phone rings. It's Brian: 'You're in deep shit.'

'What?'

'Where the hell are you?'

'I'm with Mike.'

'*Still?*' he says. 'For Christ's sake, we haven't got all day. James Merendino just called. He says if you're not over at the Grand Hotel in five minutes he's pulling out of the film.'

Jesus. Him too?

'What do you think this is, a fucking *holiday?*' says Brian.

Exactly seven minutes later I'm over at the Grand.

James is in the garden. For a moment I don't recognise him. He's shaved all his hair off. He looks like a cross between Mussolini and a boiled egg. 'Where the hell have you been?' he asks.

'Filming. I have to do that from time to time.'

'Yeah, well, now you can film me. Here I am. By the way, hello.'

'Hello, James.'

The thing about James is I'm never quite sure whether to laugh or duck. He sits at the table with two women, his girl-friend, Katrina, and his assistant, Elizabeth. Katrina is cool, dark, frighteningly self-possessed, silent where James is voluble, the sort of person who always seems to be sizing you up. Or in my case, down. I'm a little scared

174

of her. Then there's Elizabeth. From what I can gather, one of her functions is to administer to James's every whim. If he wants a cigarette (which he always does) she lights one for him. If he wants a drink, she troops off to get one. If he wants flattery, she delivers it in buckets. I'm not sure whether this is because he's paying her a huge fortune or because she really believes that James is the greatest thing since Orson Welles. Apart from that, I rather like her.

'So, James,' I say. 'You're going to pull out of the film.'

'That', he says, 'was a joke. Ha ha ha. Where's your fucking sense of humour? I've been calling your office all morning. Things are looking up. Things are looking very up. Up up up. Guess who's been calling?'

'Who?'

'I'll give you three clues. One, he's fat. Two, he's very fat.'

Christ, I think. *Stephen Loyd.*

'Three, his name begins with H.'

'Not . . . ?'

'Yes.'

'Golly.'

'He's been calling all day. Harvey Weinstein. Not me personally, of course. Cassian. My agent. You remember my agent Cassian.'

Oh, indeed I do. I do I do I do. The you've-got-sausage-on-your-face-man.

'Vaguely,' I say.

'Well, that's who he's been calling. And he's coming to the screening. Tonight. Harvey Weinstein. Now whaddya think of *that?*'

What *do* I think of that?

'I thought you said you wanted to get the guy to punch you on the nose?'

175

'I did,' says James. 'But the point is, if Harvey came along and offered you a million dollars, would you turn it down? I mean, would you?'

I assume this is an academic question. Harvey isn't going to offer me a million dollars.

In any case, the phone rings. It's Brian. 'Where the hell are you?' he asks.

'I wish you wouldn't keep asking me that,' I say. 'I'm with James.'

'*Still?* Well you're in deep shit. Stephen Loyd says he's pulling out of the film if you're not at the Carlton in five minutes.'

'Bollocks.'

'What did you say?'

'I said he's probably only joking.'

'He didn't sound like he was joking to *me*. Get your ass and the crew over there *right now*. This isn't the time to be sitting around on the fucking *beach*, for Christ's sake!'

Then he hangs up.

It's becoming obvious to me that my authority as a director has suffered considerably since that thing with Erick Zonca.

Over at the Carlton, Stephen and Gordon are busy knocking on doors. That is to say, they're cold-calling. Cold-calling usually means going into people's offices uninvited and asking them politely to consider a proposal. Mostly, you get chucked out. Occasionally, you get five minutes. Once in a million years you even make a deal. This doesn't happen with Stephen and Gordon. Part of the problem is Stephen's habit of yelling in people's faces. Plus he tends to argue with Gordon in the middle of the pitch. Also, he has a disconcerting habit of scratching his testicles at odd moments.

176

As a result, things go rapidly from bad to worse. (For them, I mean, not for me. For me they go from good to fantastic to is-this-really-happening?) Finally we get to this:

INT. DAY. OFFICE OF MAJOR US DISTRIBUTOR, CARLTON HOTEL.

Gordon is in the middle of the two-minute version of the pitch. He has already done the sixty-second and the thirty-second versions. He delivers each version in a completely expressionless monotone, although his timings are now atomic accurate. An American acquisitions executive listens impassively.

GORDON
So that's when Killer tells Rupert he's actually the nerd of the gang because as I was saying Rupert's just smoked himself unconscious on a giant bong called The Lord a bong you see is like a four-foot bit of drainpipe that you smoke the spliff through and as I was saying –

STEPHEN
(*interrupting*)
Right that's enough. We've got to go.

GORDON
Go?

ACQUISITIONS EXECUTIVE
Go?

STEPHEN
To the match.

ACQUISITIONS EXECUTIVE
The match?

177

STEPHEN

The Cup Final. Arsenal v Newcastle. Kick-off's in ten minutes.

Three nanoseconds later they're gone.

The FA Cup Final is one of the great traditions of the Cannes Film Festival, along with the Competition, the red carpet, the *Palme d'Or* and the septuagenarian transvestite who plies his trade every night opposite the Carlton Hotel. Every single Brit in town makes a beeline for the nearest TV set. Business meetings are emptied, cancelled or interrupted (as above). For many years cynics said this was one reason why the British film industry was in such a mess. Its recent renaissance has effectively disproved this theory since every Brit in town still makes a beeline for the nearest TV set. All the pavilions in town cater for the Cup Final. The British Pavilion is always packed to the gills. Second best is the Variety Pavilion, which offers a big TV screen and free booze (but no Ray-Bans). This is where Stephen and Gordon go. All the Brits – from the biggest names in the film business down to . . . well, down to Stephen and Gordon – huddle together in one jolly democratic fraternity. This is probably the only time in Cannes when what matters is not who you are or where you're staying (the Carlton or the camp site?) but which team do you support? The Americans look on, bemused. Meanwhile, Stephen sticks his bare feet on a table, bites the top off the first of several bottles of Heineken, and happily reverts to type. Outside, the traffic hums along the Croisette, the deal-making continues, the fashionable and the famous get on with the daily grind of being fashionable and famous. But here, in the Variety Pavilion, we're firmly back in Leytonstone.

Newcastle lose two–nil. For a moment I think Stephen is going to burst into tears. At any rate, this is clearly the absolute nadir of his Cannes experience so far. Or maybe it's the beer. Whatever the case, he suddenly drops a new bombshell. He's got a meeting. Not a cold-calling, knock-on-the-door, can-we-pitch-you-an-idea sort of meeting. But a meeting meeting. One that's been *arranged*. One that starts in . . . ten minutes.

The meeting is with Wendy Streich. Wendy Striech is one of those no-shit New Yorkers with a tattoo on her left breast who runs a distribution company called Manga Films. It transpires Gordon has shown her bits of his documentary *They Call It Acid* and she likes it. She may even buy it. Now she wants to hear about *Amsterdam*. And she wants to meet Stephen.

CUT TO:

EXT. DAY. BALCONY OF MAJESTIC HOTEL.

Wendy Streich is sitting at a table. Stephen and Gordon enter camera left. Both of them are pissed.

STEPHEN
(*to camera*)

Fuck off.

(*to Wendy*)

Fucking Newcastle. They fucking lost. You must be Wendy Mango.

WENDY

Wendy Streich. And it's Manga Films. With an A.

STEPHEN

Whatever. Do you want to see my ingrowing toenails? Look, I'll show you. Aren't they horrible?

He takes his trainers off. These are the same trainers he has worn since leaving England. Then he sticks a bare foot in Wendy's face. She affects to find this endearing but it's not easy when you've got a face full of toenails.

WENDY
(addressing Stephen's foot)

So. Tell me all about your movie.

CUT TO:

INT. DAY. WENDY'S SUITE. LATER.

STEPHEN

This is the script as I wrote it. There's no scene numbers, there's no running time and about five to ten per cent of the whole thing doesn't make any sense whatsoever.

He hands her a copy. On the cover there is a giant muddy boot print.

That's where the cop trod on it.

CUT TO:

INT. DAY. WENDY'S SUITE. LATER.

Wendy, Stephen and Gordon watch Stephen's trailer. Wendy looks totally impassive. Gordon looks asleep. Stephen scratches his balls.

> WENDY
>
> Never never never never ever show that to anybody ever again if you want them to put money in your movie.

CUT TO:

INT. DAY. WENDY'S SUITE. LATER.

> STEPHEN
>
> If I don't sell this script, I'm declaring bankruptcy. I've paid for this whole fucking trip.

> GORDON
> *(suddenly wakes up)*
> You haven't paid for this whole fucking trip.

> STEPHEN
> Who sorted out the van and all the stickers?

> GORDON
> You're paying for nothing.

> STEPHEN
> Nothing?

> GORDON
> Nothing.

> STEPHEN
> Nothing?

181

GORDON

You're paying for shit.

STEPHEN

I'm paying *for shit?*

Wendy's face. Are they going to start fighting in the middle of her suite?

Afterwards, Stephen says, 'I think she liked us.' Then he goes off to be sick.

*

6.30 p.m. I've shot a million feet of film so far. At this rate it will take me five years to edit this film. I've got to be more careful. Now we're off to the Grand again. James Merendino's screening is in two hours. I want to be there for Harvey. At last – my big opportunity to say hello. His big opportunity to be in my film. It's a marriage made in heaven.

By the time I arrive, James is having supper. By which I mean Elizabeth feeds him bits of *spaghetti vongole* from a soup spoon. Occasionally, she lights a cigarette for him and puts it between his lips. Katrina sits, cool and impassive as ever. But not James. James is furious. James is *fuming*. And not, this time, with me. With . . . *Cassian.* 'As from tomorrow,' he yells, 'Cassian is *dead!*' And he stabs his fork into the table-cloth.

This, of course, is music to my ears. For two reasons: (a) if James does to Cassian what he has just done to the table-cloth I will definitely win an Oscar and (b) if James does to Cassian what he has just done to the tablecloth I won't have to do it myself.

From this point on, James and I are best buddies.

182

The reason why James wants to kill Cassian is because he thinks Cassian has just killed his movie. Let me be specific. James's campaign to sell *SLC Punk* has always rested on one immovable, unalterable premise: that nobody has seen, is seeing, or will see the movie before tonight. That nobody also includes Harvey Weinstein. Thirty minutes before we got here, Cassian invited Harvey to watch the movie – *on his own* – at the same time as it's publicly screened tonight. So what? So *everything*. So Harvey is immediately *empowered*. So Harvey is separated from the industry herd. So Harvey is provided with his own special screening room to make up his own mind in his own time in his own way, a privilege granted to nobody else. To any outsider this might seem perfectly reasonable, given the guy's stature. To James, well versed in the machinations of Hollywood power games, it's the end of the world. And since Cassian is the instigator of this terrible crime, Cassian must be punished. Without mercy. Without redress. And by tomorrow latest.

'But why not tonight?' I enquire (a little too eagerly).

'Tonight?' asks James. 'Tonight is not appropriate. Tonight is my screening. Tonight, I put on my . . . Hollywood face.'

'And Cassian?'

'Cassian?' James smiles. 'I'll probably shake his hand, slap him on the back, that sort of thing. Then I'll fire him.' He gets up from the table. 'As of now, Cassian does not fucking *exist* as an agent. Not that agents exist.'

7.40 p.m. We are in James's car on the way to the screening. Elizabeth is there, Katrina is there, I am there with my camera. James wears a suit several sizes too big. Elizabeth feeds him a cigarette, his seventh in the last hour. He is obviously extremely nervous. He says, 'Maybe nobody will turn up,' or 'Maybe nobody will laugh,' or 'Maybe my mom will buy the movie.' The car turns a corner, crosses a street, pulls up outside a cinema. A few TV crews huddle in the lobby. One or two photographers. Also my crew. Perhaps thirty or forty people. So far, nobody else. But there's still twenty minutes before the screening.

7.55 p.m. Five minutes to go. More people arrive by the second, including James's mum. She looks very sweet, very neat and very out of place. Every time we turn the camera on her she hides behind a pillar. James stands by himself.

*

7.58 p.m. Two minutes left. Now we're inside the cinema. Cassian arrives. I recognise him immediately. Does he also recognise me? He says, 'Have we met before?'

I say no. Never. Not that I recall.

He peers at me for a split-second longer than a moment, then turns towards James. 'Great suit,' he says.

'Do you think?' says James. They shake hands. They clap each other on the back.

Cassian says, 'I'm going to go and work the crowds outside.' Then he says, 'Harvey's gonna love this movie. Trust me.' He exits camera left.

James looks straight down the lens of my camera. 'Tomorrow he's a dead man,' he says.

8.01 p.m. The house lights dim. The theatre is perhaps three-quarters full. James sits in the very front row, next to his mum. The screen comes alive, the story begins. The last thing

I see is James, coiled up in his seat, laughing at his own movie.
Well, it *is* a comedy after all.

10.23 p.m. The movie is over. The crowd stand in the foyer,
waiting for their cars. Several people slap James on the back.
(Cassian is one of them.) A few shake his hand. Someone
says to him, 'It was just amazing! It hit every single one of the
right buttons!'

'Oh, thank you thank you thank you,' says James, like a
stuck record.

I collar him afterwards. 'Do you think they liked it?'

'They say they *loved* it.'

'That's great.'

'No, it isn't. It's Hollywood.'

✻

Afterwards, there's the party. This is held in one of the grand
pavilions opposite the Carlton. Punk music belts out at full
throttle over the Croisette. We stop for a pizza and turn up
fifteen minutes late to find . . . that Harvey Weinstein has
been and gone. He was here for five minutes. Three minutes
with James, two with Cassian. And now the rumour mills are
spinning out of control. Questions whip round the party
like a forest fire. Did Harvey like the movie? Did Harvey *love*
the movie? Did Harvey *hate* the movie but wants the world to
think that he loved it? Did Harvey *love* the movie but wants the
world to *think* he hated it by *pretending* that he loved it? Every
possible permutation is discussed. The one thing on which
everyone agrees is that whatever else Harvey came for, it
wasn't the music.

And I . . . I missed the whole damn thing.

SUNDAY, 17 MAY, CANNES

'You *what?*' says Brian.

'You *missed* him?' says Pascale.

'Yes,' I say.

'You missed *Harvey Weinstein?*'

'Yes.'

'Jesus Christ. How the hell did you fucking *miss* him?'

'We, er, got held up. In traffic, that is.'

For a moment, nobody says anything.

'The traffic was really terrible,' I add.

Pascale and Brian look at each other in astonishment. I know that look. That look is the why-the-fuck-did-we-hire-this-guy look. That look is the how-the-hell-did-we-ever-get-in-this-fucking-mess look. Then they both look at me. I know that look too. That look is . . . that look is the same look James gave the tablecloth when he stabbed his fork into it.

'I suppose you'd better tell him about Zonca,' says Brian.

'Zonca?' I ask.

'You remember the guy? The guy you managed to piss off on Day Two.'

'Oh. Him. Yes.'

'Well,' says Pascale, 'he's agreed to be in the film again.'

'He has? That's great news. That's wonderf –'

'But there's one condition. That *you* don't go anywhere near him.'

Back in the crew van, I find everyone is taking bets on how soon I'm going to be fired. Dave gives it two days. Carl gives it three. Hannah says tomorrow. If I'm lucky. I stare out of the window.

Our first stop is Mike Hakata. He and Rolf have now got themselves an office on the Croisette. Let me start that again.

He and Rolf have now hijacked two public phone boxes on the Croisette which they're calling their office. In order to stop members of the general public from trying to use the phone, they've stuck a big sign on the windows which says TWO BAD MICE OFFICE. THIS IS NOT A PUBLIC PHONE. This doesn't actually stop members of the public from trying to use the phone at all. It just makes them angry. As a result, every phone conversation Mike and Rolf have is constantly interrupted by people banging on the window.

Somewhere in the middle of all this, Peter Johnston arrives. Peter is the combat-geared, hobnail-booted, spraycan-armed, self-styled publicity terrorist whose job is to put *Two Bad Mice* on the map of Cannes. He carries a bucket full of chalk and several Tesco bags full of indelible spray. Tonight, he plans to hit the town. By tomorrow, the words TWO BAD MICE will be ingrained on everybody's consciousness (and on a sizeable number of their foreheads). His timing is deliberate, because tomorrow is ... Mike's First Screening.

Not a flashy affair, this. Not the sort of screening James Merendino had last night. And several light-years away from the sort of screening Erick Zonca is going to have tonight. But a screening nevertheless. In the Bunker. Eighty seats. If Mike can get the buyers to come he's got a chance to sell his movie. That's if they bother to stay.

'We've got our campaign all sorted,' says Mike. 'Fuck *Godzilla*.'

'What?'

'Fuck *Godzilla*. That's our campaign. What do you think?'

'Fuck *Godzilla*?'

'Yup. By tomorrow it'll be all over this town. Basically, we're head to head with *Godzilla* now.'

'What was the budget for *Godzilla*?'

187

'About two hundred million.'

'What's your budget?'

'About twenty grand.' He gets up. 'Oh, shit,' he says. 'Someone's using my office.'

By lunch-time I'm over at the Grand Hotel with James. He's in the middle of a whole series of interviews. Most of them are with German TV, since – like us – the Germans have put lots of money into *SLC Punk*. Unlike us, James actually *did* put a German in his film and he's here right now. His name is Til Schweiger. He's supposed to be rather famous and a bit of a heart-throb but to me he looks like a war veteran. He's blond and he's blue-eyed, he's in perfect physical shape and all the female interviewers swoon behind their cameras, damn him. They don't swoon with James. (Not with that haircut.) They just read him questions from a prepared list.

CUT TO:

EXT. DAY. GARDENS OF THE GRAND HOTEL.

A middle-aged German TV interviewer with enormous spectacles and a very serious expression sits opposite James.

MIDDLE-AGED GERMAN TV INTERVIEWER

I am especially interested in the philosophical aspects of your film. Could you perhaps elaborate on these a little bit?

JAMES

The philosophical aspects of the film?

(*Long pause*)

Um . . .

(*Very long pause*)

Er . . .
Um . . .

Apart from the philosophical aspects of the film (which consists largely of people yelling at each other) James is asked over and over again whether it's also autobiographical. Each time he says no. Instantly I'm reminded of Malcolm Muggeridge's classic TV interview with the writer Robert Graves:

MUGGERIDGE: Your love poems have an immediacy which makes one think they must be based on real people. Is this actually so, or are they entirely creatures of your imagination?

GRAVES: Are you asking for telephone numbers?

After half an hour I get James all to myself. No more crap about the philosophical aspects of his film. I have just two questions: simple, straight and right to the point. Question Number One:
  'What about Harvey?'
  'What *about* Harvey?'
  'He came to the party last night.'
  'He did. You missed it.'
  'We got stuck in traffic.'
  'Traffic?'
  'Traffic.'
  'I didn't see any traffic.'
  Get back to the point, Stephen. 'Did he like the movie?'

189

'He said it was a work of genius.'

'He said that?'

'Listen,' says James. 'It means nothing. It means shit. So Harvey comes to the party. So what? It happens all the time in Hollywood.'

'This isn't Hollywood.'

'This is Hollywood,' says James. 'A super-concentrated-tomato-paste version of Hollywood. Look. It means nothing. There's no deal. There's no offer. Not yet. Maybe never. We'll see.'

Question Number Two: 'Is Cassian dead?'

'Er – well – not *exactly*,' he says. He brandishes his wrist at me. Where yesterday there was nothing on it, today there is a very expensive-looking watch. 'Cassian gave it to me this morning. It's a Bulgari. Apparently, it's worth seven thousand five hundred dollars.'

'Seven thousand five hundred dollars?'

'That's what Cassian says.' He holds the watch to his ear. 'How the hell am I supposed to fire him when he gives me a seven-thousand-five-hundred-dollar watch?'

'I don't know,' I say. But what I'm really thinking is, you should row with your agent more often.

10.15 p.m. I'm writing this in the car. Twenty minutes ago Erick Zonca went up the red carpet into the Palais for the screening of his movie. I watched the whole thing from a café across the street. For a director, this is the equivalent of not getting it up. To witness the central event in the life of one of your characters and not direct it is a horribly humiliating experience. But what can I do? The guy doesn't want me there. And the last thing I want to do right now is blow the whole story. So I sit in the café, and watch and wonder, as the most astonishing spectacle of success unfolds in front of me.

This is how Cannes honours its gods. This is what it looks like to be at the Top of the Tree.

There are twenty-two red-carpeted steps from ground to entrance. Not very many, really. It takes maybe thirty seconds for an ordinary mortal to climb them on an ordinary day. But this isn't an ordinary day. And Zonca isn't an ordinary mortal. He's a *realisateur*, he's an *auteur*, he's France's answer to Ken Loach, he's the next Truffaut and he's got a movie — *a first movie* — in Competition. As a result, he takes at least ten minutes to climb all twenty-two steps. Ten minutes in which he's filmed, photographed, cheered, worshipped, by batteries of paparazzi, cameramen, report- ers, fans, tourists, cineastes, cinephiles and Festival officials. He moves from step to step, occasionally pausing for the photographers, his two actresses and Virginie by his side. The actresses are both beautiful, one dark, one blonde, the blonde in particular, a face of rapture turning first to Zonca, then to the photographers, then to the crowds, then back to Zonca . . . Even from my café across the road I see this. And I wonder (oh, how I wonder) what all this must *mean* to him. He is no fool. He knows as well as everyone — better than everyone, perhaps — that this orgy of adulation may be the first and last in his life. After all, nobody has seen the movie yet. It could be a disaster. They might all hate it. In another three hours he may exit the Palais to . . . nobody. To an embarrassed silence. At best (or at worst), to desultory applause. I remember when I met Zonca in Paris he said he hated the very idea of Cannes. The very idea of Cannes is an easy thing to hate when you're a failure. But when you're a success, when you've won . . . then, perhaps, hate isn't part of the equation. And watching Zonca now, watching him smile and laugh and wave, watching him throw private, conspiratorial glances to Virginie and to his actresses, I wonder again what it is he must be feeling. Is it exhilaration? Wonder? Bemusement? Incredulity? Or is it fear?

As for me, I sit in the café and watch. From a technical point of view this is a fantastically complex scene. Only one bite at the cherry. Only limited resources (e.g. *no director*). We have three camera units. The Festival insists on fixed positions, behind the barriers which line each side of the stairs. These positions are booked days in advance. Once the camera is set up, you don't move. And you can't move, because every other cameraman in town will kill you if you try. The reason is simple. This, as they say in the porno industry, is the money shot. Fuck it up and you're dead. Hence the one bite. Dave on the left side, shooting black and white. Cian, our Irish cameraman, on the right, shooting colour. Dave on a telephoto lens. Cian on a wide-angle lens. Together, they'll pick up most of the action without (we hope) being bashed over the head by the next-door neighbour. I tell Dave to train his camera directly on Zonca's face all the way from the moment he exits the car to the moment he enters the Palais. That's ten minutes, an entire roll of film. A fabulously difficult shot, but one which I know he will get. I want to see every shade of emotion in Zonca's face, every subtle, fleeting expression as it is felt in the instant that it is felt. Cian's job is to capture the whole scene, the *bigness* of the moment, as it happens. Two superb cameramen, two angles, two very different challenges. But we also have a joker up our sleeve. And that joker is Alan.

Alan's job is to pretend he isn't a cameraman at all. He poses as a friend of Zonca. This means he goes up the steps with Zonca, as one of the party, one of the blessed. The fact that he also happens to have his camera with him – one of those lovely little brilliantly polished Super 8 gems — is neither here nor there. He's making a home movie. For Zonca. His status, in other words, is unofficial. If our little gag works it means he won't be tied behind a barrier, rooted to a position. It means he can roam and wander at will. It means, in other words, he'll be able to get the most remarkable and unique images ever captured of this remarkable and unique event. A billion-dollar money shot.

That's the plan. Amazingly, Zonca has agreed to play along. Perhaps it appeals to the director in him. Maybe his mind is on other things. Or possibly Pascale has worked her little bit of magic. I don't know. At any rate, Alan gets out of the car after Zonca. Like everybody else, he's in evening dress. His shoes are polished, his hair is brushed, his shirt is crisp and clean and white . . . and he's holding the camera in his hand. He looks like . . . exactly what he's not supposed to look like. He looks like a *cameraman*. All the other cameramen, the ones behind the barriers, the ones who booked their positions six weeks ago, the ones who can't move for fear of being murdered, stare in astonishment as Alan whirls round and round Zonca, totally fucking up their shot. And fucking up their shot — *this* shot — means, as we know, certain death. It means instant execution, without redress. Everybody starts to yell at Alan. I can hear it from the café. They shout, they scream, they curse in a thousand languages. And Alan ignores them all. Up up the steps he goes, higher and higher, whirling and twirling round Zonca (his trademark is *cinematic fluidity*) pointing his dinky little camera this way and that, capturing for all time the billion-volt moment with the billion-dollar money shot. I hold my breath. Everything depends on this. My movie depends on this. My career depends on this. *My Oscar* depends on . . .

193

And then, suddenly, just three short steps before the very top, Alan is stopped. By which I mean he's grabbed from behind and nearly strangled. By which I mean he's dead.

Well, not *dead* exactly. But dead – professionally. To be specific, now I am in possession of all the facts. These are:

(1) That Alan, on first being stopped, turned round to his attacker and yelled, 'GET THE FUCK OFF ME YOU FUCKING C**T!'

(2) That the man to whom he said and did this was, in fact, a very senior officer of the Cannes Film Festival.

And that, as a direct consequence of (1) and (2):

(3) We are now banned from the Cannes Film Festival for ever.

MONDAY, 18 MAY, CANNES

Despite the best preparations, despite the most careful planning, the one certain rule about film-making, the one absolute guarantee, is that everything always goes wrong. Let me repeat that. Everything. Always. Goes. Wrong. There are people who say that filming is an exhilarating, creatively rewarding experience. They say it's spiritually fulfilling. They say how lucky we are somebody actually *pays* us to do this job. They say it's better than sex. This, of course, is bollocks. Filming is about lurching from one crisis to another. Filming is about trying not to drown when the waves crash over your head. Filming is about survival when all the odds are stacked against you. Filming is about desperately not wanting to be filming. Especially right now.

Especially right now. To all intents and purposes we are dead. Look at the facts. We are bankrupt, professionally, journalistically, financially. The figures speak for themselves. We have, in effect, written off almost half a million pounds. In the book of professional sins, this is probably the worst. Let me rephrase that. In the book of professional sins, this is *definitely* the worst. When I started this job, ten years ago, I thought people really cared if a film was good or bad. I thought it actually *mattered*. And so it does – to me, to a few punters, possibly to one or two of my peers. But to the Great and the Good in the industry, the simple truth is ... it doesn't matter at all. Fuck up a film, turn out a piece of trash, make a balls-up of the whole thing ... and nobody gives a damn. But screw up over the *money* ... and it's another story. The money is everything! The money is *it*! And what we're talking about here is a lot of money. A frightening amount of money.

Is there life after death? That is the question facing us now. First, can we even complete the film? Second, can we throw ourselves at the feet of the Festival, go down on our hands and knees and beg for mercy? Third, who – of all of us – is the best person to do that? (There's also a fourth question, namely, when do we castrate Alan, but right now nobody seems to know where he is.) The answers, in order, are (i) yes – just, (ii) yes and (iii) please God not me.

This is when Pascale really starts to earn her fee. She gets on the phone, calls up one of her contacts at the Festival Office. Within five minutes she manages to get an appointment with the guy Alan pissed off. The appointment is at noon. Everything hangs on it. She spends the next couple of hours practising different ways of grovelling in front of the mirror. Then she leaves.

As for me, I have work to do. Despite the banning, there are still places I can film. All the hotels, restaurants, pavilions, offices and the Palais are out of bounds. But that still leaves the beach, the street and the odd bar. It's not much, but it's something. Enough to carry on. Call it the Dunkirk spirit. Or call it naked terror. In the end it comes down to the same thing. Keep going.

My first appointment is with Stephen and Gordon. One of our backers, Dieter Kosslick, has asked to meet them. This is not the sort of request you refuse when one of your backers makes it. This is also not the sort of request your refuse when one of your backers is just about to find out he's lost several hundred thousand of his Deutschmarks by backing your film. Not that I tell him that, of course. For one thing it would be impolitic. For another I'm far too scared.

Dieter Kosslick is a flamboyant character, well-known on the Cannes circuit. He runs a German Film Foundation with a title I've never been able to get my tongue round: the Nord-Rhein Westphalien Filmstiftung. His budget is $20 million. He is trim, lean, neat, successful and very likeable. He is also . . . very German. By which I mean he displays, I think deliberately, *all* the stereotypical national characteristics. He is ordered, correct, bureaucratic, sensible, efficient. He is, in other words, everything that Stephen and Gordon are not. This makes for an interesting culture clash. To wit:

EXT. CAFÉ. DAY.

Stephen and Gordon sit at a table opposite Dieter Kosslick. Stephen reads an

196

excerpt from his script at very high speed in broad East London minicab-speak. Dieter tries to keep up.

STEPHEN

Jimmy stares nervously at Killer . . . Listen I've got to go cos there's a pub quiz down the Albert and I wanna get a few things done. Yeah no problem. Killer hurries off. Bollocks. Charlie gets a fag out and puts it in his mouth, pats his pocket searching for a lighter. Fifty pee. Jimmy stops and looks around. An Asian man is standing in the news kiosk holding up a disposable lighter. Fifty pee or two for a quid. Jimmy drifts over to the kiosk staring at the man. Jimmy slowly smiles at the man and takes the fag —

Dieter listens. From his expression it is clear he doesn't have the slightest clue what any of this is about. Neither do I.

CUT TO:

EXT. CAFÉ. DAY. AN HOUR LATER.

STEPHEN

Like I said there's no scene numbers, there's no running time and there's still about five to ten per cent of the actual script that doesn't make sense (*Dieter's expression: 99.9 per cent of the actual script doesn't make sense*) but once the finances are in place the first thing that happens is the script goes to a professional ghost writer so they can like clean it up sort of thing and . . .

DIETER
(*Confused*)

Clean it up?

197

Yeah. Clean it up. You know. Make it industry spec.

DIETER
(*Seriously confused*)

Industry spec?

CUT TO:

EXT. CAFÉ. DAY. TWO HOURS LATER.

Stephen is still talking. Dieter looks exhausted.

STEPHEN
I've got another script. It started out as *Italia 2 The German Job.*

DIETER
The German Job?

STEPHEN
Yeah. Like *The Italian Job.*

DIETER
The Italian Job?

STEPHEN
The Italian Job. Michael Caine. With the minis. So I wrote a sequel a couple of years back called *Italia 2 The German Job* and it was a heist that was set in Germany you know bunch of East End villains do a Brinks Matt bullion job twenty-six million nicker huge great big car chase on the autobahn but Paramount have decided that as far as *The Italian Job* is concerned they're going to remake the original which I think is a big mistake because like with . . .

Dieter's face. There is no escape.

Afterwards Stephen says, 'I think he liked us.'

'He definitely liked us,' says Gordon.

'And he loved the script,' says Stephen.

'He definitely loved the script,' says Gordon.

'And he's got twenty million to blow,' says Stephen.

'A couple more days like this,' says Gordon, 'and we can set fire to the van.'

'Next year,' says Stephen gazing out to sea. 'I'm going to get me a great big yacht.'

We're packing up the camera when the phone rings. It's Pascale. 'Do you want the good news or the bad news?' she asks.

'The bad news.'

'The bad news is that Alan is hereby forbidden to go within five hundred metres of the Palais for the rest of his natural life.'

'And the good news . . . ?'

A pause. 'The good news is that we're . . . OK. We're in. We can go on. We are back in business, baby.'

A huge wave of relief floods over me. For a moment I can't speak.

'Well?' she demands.

'Pascale,' I answer. 'You are a fucking genius.'

'I know,' she says. 'I am.'

This evening we celebrate. Brian takes the whole team out to a restaurant by the marina. We eat lobsters, we drink champagne. A warm breeze spools off the sea. A million lights hang over the city. People in evening dress wander past our table. Music drifts across the bay. Out on the Croisette, the world gathers in the bars, the cafés, the restaurants, before going on to a thousand parties. Over at the Palais a new set of actors play out last night's game to the same fans,

199

the same cheers, the same carefully orchestrated ritual of success. And so it goes on, night after night, until the end of the Festival. And we sit at our table, and talk, and wonder, and sip champagne, and feel the warmth of the soft night air.

And for the first time since coming here, I am content.

✵   ✵   ✵

Last night I dreamt I kept getting all my characters mixed up. I rush off to film Mike Hakata at the Palais. He is climbing the red steps. Millions of people surround him . . . Hundreds of photographers call out to him. He sees me in the crowd and winks. Suddenly I am in the yellow van. Erick Zonca is driving. He speaks like a minicab driver. He says over his shoulder, 'We got done by the fucking gendarmerie last night' and I wonder what it is that he has done. Out of the window I see Stephen Loyd wearing a dinner suit. He sits at a table in the most expensive restaurant in Cannes. A waiter serves him plates of oysters. I suddenly realise the waiter is Harvey Weinstein. I try to get Erick to stop the van but it isn't Erick who's driving it now, it's James. He says, 'You'd have to be Stevie Wonder or Ray fucking Charles not to notice this,' but I don't know what he's talking about. I keep thinking I ought to ask him about his movie but I can't remember the title. I can't even remember what it is about. Suddenly I am gripped by a terrible panic. Who are these people? Why am I here? What am I supposed to ask them? The van passes the Palais again. This time it is raining. Thousands of umbrellas line the steps. The rain beats down on the red carpet. The wind howls. Someone is walking up the steps, battling against the wind, but I don't recognise him. I know I know him but I don't recognise him . . . Is it Mike again? Is it Zonca? Is it Stephen? Is it James? Once again the panic builds. Who is he? What is he doing there? The figure turns towards me, smiles, winks and disappears. Only then do I realise that it is actually me.

TUESDAY, 19 MAY, CANNES

In the shower this morning I listen to the radio. Cannes, as always, dominates the news. A reporter delivers his verdict on the movies so far. *La Vita è Bella* – that's Roberto Benigni's film – gets a big tick. So does John Boorman's *The General*. One or two others get the big thumbs down. But the number one story is Erick Zonca. *La Vie Revée des Anges*, it seems, is the hit of the Festival. Right now the rumour buzzing round town is that Zonca is tipped to win the Festival's greatest and most prestigious prize – the *Palme d'Or*.

This is extraordinary, for two reasons: (i) Because the *Palme d'Or*, in the entire history of the Cannes Film Festival, has hardly ever been won by a first-time director. And (ii) because the first I get to hear of it is on the radio. This is a damning indictment of our relationship with the guy. By which I mean this is damning proof that there *is no* relationship with the guy. All I feel is frustration. Here I am, sitting on an explosive story and I can't get near it. I can't touch it. The man hates my guts. Even Pascale finds him hard going. On the surface, they get on perfectly well. But getting on perfectly well isn't the point. The point is to probe him, to bring him out, to open him up, to dissect him – and all before he's realised it's even happened. This is the mark of a great interviewer. To be all sorts of things at once: to be father confessor, therapist, journalist, cross-examiner and surgeon. It's a very difficult skill. It requires fantastic patience. It also requires an instinct for predicting the next move, an uncanny sense of what the other person is thinking almost before he thinks it. I'm not at all sure I have it. But I'm certain Pascale doesn't.

On the credit side . . . well, it's something if one of our four characters actually wins the *Palme d'Or*. At the very least, we'll have got something right. The gamble will have paid off. And the spectacle is . . . *spectacular*. By which I mean every one of the 2400 seats in the Palais will be filled with the great and the good and the gorgeous in the movie business. This time, it's not just Zonca going up the red steps. *Everybody* goes up. The crowds will be huge, thousands, possibly tens of thousands of people, spreading out beyond the Palais enclosure, out into the streets, out even to the beach. Every photographer, cameraman and reporter will be there in force. The *Palmares* — as it is called — is the climax of the Festival, Cannes's answer to the World Heavyweight Boxing Championship, the moment when all the gladiators step into the ring at the same time and battle it out for the title. Who will win? Who will be the champion? Who will be the Greatest of Them All? In just four days, we will know.

But that's then. This is now. And now is . . . Mike's First Screening. This is in an eighty-seat theatre in the Palais. All week he's been in his office, running through several hundred phone cards in an effort to get people to come. The phone box is a mess of papers, Post-Its, broken pencils, fag butts. Nobody bangs on the windows any more. There's no point. Mike is never coming out. His movie depends on it. His *life* depends on it. Everything he's ever done in the last three years, all the frustration, the struggle, the madness, the pain, the exhilaration, is zeroed into this one moment, this point, this *now*. Meanwhile, Peter — his publicity terrorist — has been machine-gunning indelible spray all over Cannes. Everywhere *Godzilla* is being Fucked. On pavements, on walls, on buildings, the legend is there, brassy and bold. This morning, I popped into the loo of the Majestic. A man in a suit was trying to wash FUCK GODZILLA SEE TWO BAD MICE off his forehead. No chance, mate.

202

10.45 a.m. One hour and fifteen minutes before the screening. I meet Mike outside his phone box. He hasn't slept for three days. He looks awful. His eyeballs stick out like golfballs. I ask him if he's nervous. 'Nervous?' He laughs. 'Nervous? I'm not nervous at all. *At all.*'

10.47 a.m. Mike lights a cigarette.

10.49 a.m. Mike lights another cigarette.

10.51 a.m. Mike lights another cigarette.

10.54 a.m. Mike lights another cigarette.

10.59 a.m. Mike lights two cigarettes at the same time.

11.26 a.m. Mike runs out of cigarettes.

11.27 a.m. Mike panics.

11.45 a.m. Fifteen minutes before the screening. Forty, maybe fifty people have turned up. Mike is interviewed by Egyptian TV, the only news crew there. The interviewer asks Mike to name his all-time favourite Egyptian movie. Mike says he needs to think about that one.

11.54 a.m. Mike is still thinking.

11.57 a.m. Mike is still thinking. The Egyptian crew pack up and leave.

11.59 a.m. The cinema doors close. A last head count. More than sixty people have turned up. Mike is exuberant.

12.01 p.m. Mike's movie begins.

Mike's movie begins . . . without Mike. 'I couldn't stand it,' he says. 'I've watched it a million times. I'm sick of the bloody thing. Let's get a drink.'

We exit the Palais, into the fresh air. Mike is strung out like razor-wire, a coiled-up, packed-in, sprung-tight, nicotine-fuelled, electrified mass of pure fear. We sit in a café across the street, while he counts the minutes before the film ends and smokes all my fags. I switch on my camera. Mike says, 'Three years ago, this wasn't part of my fucking deal. Three years ago, this was an idea me and my mates were going to put on fucking VHS. And now . . .' He looks over at the Palais, at the tourists strolling in the sun. 'And now, we're here, in Cannes, in the Palais, and they're actually showing . . . *my movie.*'

For a moment neither of us speaks.

'Do you think they'll buy it?' I ask finally.

'Do I think they'll buy it?' He pauses a moment. Then he says, 'You know, it's something just to be here. Even if nobody buys it. Even if they hate the fucking movie. Just to be here is really . . . something. For me.'

The result of Mike's first screening is that . . . nobody buys the movie. Not yet, anyway. True to the best traditions in the movie business, everybody says, 'I *loved* the movie.' By which they mean they didn't love the movie enough to buy it there and then. By which they mean they're waiting to see if anybody else wants to buy the movie. If anybody else wants to buy the movie that means the movie is probably worth buying, in which case they'll all try to buy it. If nobody else wants to buy the movie that means the movie must be shit. In other words, unless you're Harvey Weinstein or God, nobody has an opinion until somebody else has one first. This is what distributors call keeping an open mind. That way, everybody respects you for your opinion.

In the meantime, Mike is left with a hundred business cards and a hundred invitations to do lunch. Some time. Soon. In the near future. When things aren't so crazy. When things have slowed down. You know how it is. Maybe after Cannes. Maybe next year.

And what does Mike do? He carefully stacks all the business cards in a suitcase, puts the suitcase to one side, gets back to his phone box and starts all over again. It's one thirty on a sunny afternoon in Cannes, which means he's got exactly 53 hours and 45 minutes before his second — and final — screening. One hundred and eighty seats, this time. A larger cinema. A bigger campaign. A last chance.

*

In the meantime we have other things on our mind. There's a rumour spinning round town that one of the biggest porno companies is throwing a huge party tonight on a yacht. It's only a rumour, but like all rumours, this one grows and swells, and expands into one desperate fantasy of epic proportions. This isn't a party, it's . . . an *orgy*. A wild, swinging, scorching, billion-watt orgy out on the biggest yacht in the marina, fuelled by free booze, free girls, free . . . *everything*. Every male member of my crew wants to go. Since I am the director, they all ask me to fix it. As a carrot, they offer to work eighteen hours a day if I do. This isn't much of a carrot since we're already working eighteen hours a day. But there again, it might be kind of . . . interesting to see. From a professional standpoint. As it were. I agree to give it a go.

Deep down in the dark bowels of the Bunker, in a giant, air-conditioned, neon-lit hall several floors beneath the basement, the porn companies (and the horror flick companies and all the other sub-zero triple-X movies) set up shop. We descend in a lift. A couple of hundred feet above our heads is the 2400-seat Palais cinema. Up there, Erick Zonca and his like cavort with the gods. Down here there are no gods. Overweight, balding, middle-aged men in drip-dry shirts scour the hundred or so booths buying and selling and watching endless porn movies. If this reads like a cliché, that's because it *is* a cliché. The thing about this industry is that it conforms exactly to expectations. All the men are wearing fake Rolex watches, fake hair and fake gold ID bracelets. All the women are up on the screen faking orgasms. (Not that I'm watching.)

For this flip-side of the movie business, Cannes has become as important as its big respectable brother upstairs. An entire alternative festival – cheekily named the *Hot d'Or* – takes place at exactly the same time. There's even a prize-giving ceremony, a sort of low-rent mirror image of the *Palmarès*. A poster on a wall announces this year's nominees for Best Multiple Orgasm. There are also prizes for Best Anal Sex, Best Oral Sex, Best Lesbian Love Scene and something called Best Double Sandwich (which, in case you're wondering, is not an award for the best location catering). Whether all this is deliberate irony or not, I don't know. I suspect not. I suspect it's a fantastically misguided attempt to gain respectability. If they can do it, so the argument goes, why can't *we*? If I'm right, this gives me my opening gambit for tonight's (putative) party. I'm respectable. I'm Upstairs. For God's sake, I'm the BBC.

CUT TO:

INT. THE BUNKER. DAY.

A man sits at a desk in front of a blank TV screen. On the walls are lots of posters of . . . well, lots of posters. I walk boldly up to the desk, prominently displaying my BBC ID.

ME

I'm from the BBC.

(*Beat*)

The British Broadcasting Corporation.

MAN BEHIND DESK

So?

ME

So I . . . er . . . gather there's a party tonight? On a yacht? In the marina?

MAN BEHIND DESK

So?

ME

So we're, er, making a film about . . . about Alternative Cannes. A big film. A *movie*. A very important movie. A very big important movie.

MAN BEHIND DESK

So?

ME

So we'd . . . we'd be very interested in filming it. The party, I mean. For our big film. For our extremely big very important film for the BBC. If you see what I mean?

Sure.

(*He takes five invitations out of a drawer and hands them to me*)

Will five be enough?

The party starts at six thirty. At six ten we have to do an interview with Zonca's press agent. The interview is over by six thirteen. I have never seen my crew work this fast. Lights, camera, action, a couple of quick questions, interrupt the answers, cut the camera, wrap the lights and we're out of there. Five minutes later Dave, my cameraman, is putting the final touches to his *toilette*. Boiled down to basics, this entails spraying half a gallon of odiferous hair spray over his head. He wears a black suit, black tie, black shirt, black cowboy boots and black sunglasses. He looks like a hitman. He says, 'The thing about this sort of event is that you've got to look the part. I look the part. You don't.'

'I don't?'

'You don't. You haven't got a fucking clue. The fundamental difference between me and you is that I'm cool and you're not.' He checks his hair in the mirror. 'Right,' he says. 'Six twenty-five. Time to *party*.'

The porno yacht is moored at the far end of the pier. There's a double irony here. One, it's by far the biggest yacht in the marina and two, it's ever so slightly – but ever so significantly – separated from all the others. And when I say big, I mean *big*. A great gleaming white wedding-cake of a ship, with tier upon tier of decks stretching seventy-five feet up into the sky. The thing dominates every other yacht in the harbour, a deliberate, explicit, outrageous testament to the sheer size of an industry which is ten times richer than its mainstream cousin. By the time we arrive, crowds of paparazzi are standing on the pier, divided by roped-off barriers from a VIP section which leads to a gangway which leads . . . to the boat. There's even a red carpet.

We, of course, are VIPs. This means that for the first and only time in Cannes, we get the red-carpet treatment. All the other photographers, reporters and news cameramen gawp with a mixture of envy and incredulity as we flash our five invites and step easily through the barriers into the VIP section. The key now is to play the part. We have to look like what we say we are, i.e. we have to look like a BBC film crew making a Very Important Film About Alternative Cannes. Any suspicion that we're *not* making a Very Important Film About Alternative Cannes and we're out. But we have a little trick up our sleeves, a 100 per cent foolproof, tried and tested formula guaranteed to forestall all suspicion at all times. It's called 'Strawberry Filter'.

Strawberry Filter, like not paying your licence fee, is an honourable BBC tradition. It simply means pretending to film when you're not. This is obviously very useful at times. For instance, you might be obliged to film someone you don't want to film, or someone who's very boring, or someone who's very prolix . . . There are a million reasons why you might have to film someone you don't want to film and, at nearly £200 for every ten minutes, film stock is an expensive commodity. Hence the magic formula. All you do is say, 'I think we'll use the strawberry filter, Dave' and Dave conveniently forgets to run any film in the camera. It works every time. It works *this* time.

So there we are in the VIP section, all five of us, waiting to go on board, with a clapper-board re-titled 'BBC TV: Alternative Cannes', with a huge pile of lights, cameras, sound equipment, tripods, cables, with several cans of film absolutely none of which is ever going to be used. To add to the illusion, Brian pretends to make lots of important calls on three different mobile phones. Dave pretends to do a bit of general filming (the yacht, the harbour, the sunset all make interesting pretend shots), my sound recordist pretends to record and I pretend to direct. In the middle of all this, a huge shout goes up from the assembled paparazzi. The stars have arrived.

There's no mistaking them. They all have six-inch heels, they all have blonde hair, they all have silicone implants and they all have that glazed, there's-nothing-behind-my-eyes expression which I suppose is the net effect of boredom, brainlessness and several tons of cocaine. They're accompanied by several beach-blond hunks in cut-off T-shirts, but nobody is interested in *them*. One of the girls trips up over the carpet. The paparazzi yell out their names. (How do they *know* their names?) The girls turn and smile and occasionally wave to the cameras. The whole thing is a sort of penny-farthing parody of what is going on right now, at this very moment, a few hundred yards away on the steps of the Palais. We, of course, pretend to film it all.

At this point an astonishing thing happens. Before the girls board the yacht they all take off their shoes. This, apparently, is some unspoken rule. Everybody has to take off their shoes. Within five minutes the red carpet of the VIP section is stacked with a hundred pairs of six-inch, steel-tipped, stilettoed shoes, all standing in precisely ordered rows, like the inside of a shoe fetishist's cupboard. Meanwhile, the girls themselves look somehow stilted, less fantastic, more vulnerable, more . . . *ordinary*, as they stomp with stumpy legs up the gangplank and into the yacht. We follow behind. Minus, of course, our own shoes.

Let's get one thing straight from the start. It's not an orgy.

In fact, it looks disappointingly like any number of cocktail parties taking place on any number of other yachts in the harbour. The girls stand around, faintly embarrassed. The men, mostly middle-aged, stand around looking faintly frustrated. All the men are wearing ordinary clothes. The only person who isn't wearing ordinary clothes is Dave (who looks like he's wandered off the set of *The Godfather*). Meanwhile, he pretends to film. I pretend to interview. In the course of the next half-hour, I pretend to interview the director of *Lactamania 14*, the producer of *Cum Cannibals*, both male stars of *Cocks In Frocks*, all three female leads of *Wer Ficht Mich In Strumpfhosen* (one for my German backers, that – except there's no film in the camera) and the man responsible for floating the world's biggest adult entertainment company on the New York Stock Exchange. Most of these interviews are very short (a) because I'm always pretending to run out of film and (b) because I'm always actually running out of things to ask. What, for example, do you ask the female lead of *Wer Ficht Mich In Strumpfhosen*? Apart from what does it mean?

CUT TO:

EXT. PORN BOAT. EVENING.

'A' Deck. The party is in full swing. I am introduced to a fat man with a silver ponytail and a floral shirt unbuttoned to his navel. Although I do not realise it, this is actually one of the greatest porn directors of all time, the Ingmar Bergman of the adult entertainment industry.

ME

Tell me about your movies.

211

FAMOUS PORN DIRECTOR
My movies? My movies are balletic variations on the act of love,
created and designed to capture in the very instant of the act of
love the sensuous rhythms and sublimated yearnings of the final
essence of the human spirit.

ME
Er – right.

(*Pause*)

So what's your favourite?

FAMOUS PORN DIRECTOR
Wild Bananas On Butt Row 4.

ME
I think we've just run out of film.

CUT TO:

EXT. PORN BOAT. EVENING. LATER.

*'B' Deck. The party is still in full swing. I am introduced to a gorgeous
woman with strawberry-blonde hair and the sort of lipstick you can see your
own reflection in. Although I do not realise it, this is actually one of the greatest
porn stars of all time, the Ingrid Bergman of the adult entertainment industry.*

ME
Do you, er, enjoy your job?

FAMOUS PORN STAR
Oh, yes. Very much indeed.

ME

Who's your favourite director?

FAMOUS PORN STAR

My favourite director is (*she names the famous director I've just interviewed*). He is a genius. His movies are balletic variations on the act of love, created and designed to capture in the very instant of the act of love the sensuous rhythms and sublimated yearnings of the final essence of the human spirit.

ME

That's exactly what he said.

FAMOUS PORN STAR

He did?

(*She is genuinely surprised*)

Tomorrow I do another movie with him. It is called *Wild Bananas On Butt Row 5*.

ME

What part do you play?

FAMOUS PORN STAR

A wild banana.

CUT TO:

EXT. PORN BOAT. NIGHT.

'C' Deck. I am introduced to a thin, tall man in a dark-blue suit, with a patch over his left eye and a scar on his right cheek. Although I do not realise it, this is actually one of the greatest porn producers of all time, the Harvey

213

Weinstein of the adult entertainment industry. He is also the owner of the
yacht. Let's just call him . . . Chuck.

ME

(quietly, to Dave)

Strawberry filter, Dave.

CHUCK

What did you say?

ME

I'm sorry?

CHUCK

You said strawberry filter.

ME

I did?

CHUCK

Don't fuck with me. You said strawberry filter.

ME

Strawberry filter? (*Beat*) Oh, *strawberry filter*. Ha ha ha. Yes.
Indeed. It's . . . a sort of technical term we use. For the gearing.
For the lens mount gearing. For the lens mount coupled ratio T
stop distagon neutral density F number gearing.

CHUCK

The hell it is. Get the fuck off my boat.

With the assistance of two security guards we get the fuck off his boat. The
next fifteen minutes are spent trying to find our shoes.

By now it's well after midnight. The rest of the crew decide
to go to the Channel Four party, in some warehouse on the

outskirts of Cannes. 'I haven't got all dressed up like this for *nothing*,' says Dave. The others try to persuade me to go, but I've had enough for one night. And I'm tired. I'm very, very tired. So they split and drift into the crowds, and leave me to go home to bed. I turn off the Croisette, up an empty side street, back towards my hotel. Someone rushes past me. A tall figure in combat gear with boot polish on his face. He dashes across the street, leaps over a barrier, swerves round a corner, and disappears. It's exactly forty-three hours before Mike Hakata's final screening and all over town Peter Johnston – his publicity terrorist – is out fucking *Godzilla*. He's even sprayed the walls of my hotel.

WEDNESDAY, 20 MAY, CANNES

INT. HOTEL BEDROOM. LATE MORNING.

The room is a tip. Despite the fact I've been here for a week, nothing is unpacked. Ashtrays overflowing with cigarette butts lie on the table. Dirty underpants lie on the floor. The sun streams through the windows. I am fast asleep, still in my clothes.

FX the phone. It's Brian.

BRIAN

Where the fuck are you?

ME
(half asleep)

Having wild sex with a gorgeous blonde.

BRIAN

Having *what?* You're supposed to be with James, for Christ's sake!

ME

I am?

BRIAN

You are. Get your ass over to the Grand. James is waiting. He's got some . . . *news*.

ME

What news?

BRIAN

You'll see.

*

'Harvey Weinstein is about to make me an offer,' says James.

We're sitting at a table in the garden: Elizabeth, Katrina, James, me.

'What offer?'

'We don't know. Maybe a two-picture deal.'

'What's a two-picture deal?'

'A two-picture deal', explains James, 'is a fuck of a lot of money.'

Two-picture or three-picture deals, I learn, are a staple diet in Hollywood. Their function is simple: to enslave, to entrap, to bond. They are a means of ownership, a way of ensuring a director works for you and not the other guy. The reward is lucre. The penalty is . . . loss of freedom. To somebody like James, that freedom is everything. Of course, it also means having to raise money from soft-porn entrepreneurs, born-again Christians and Mafia organisations. But that's the ace in his hand. By playing off one lot of born-again Christians against another lot of pornographers, he ends up with *his* movie. Not theirs. Harvey Weinstein, on the

216

other hand, is a different ball game. He's a movie producer. He owns one of the biggest movie production companies in the business. Once you sign a two-picture deal, you give up your rights. Soul and body, you are *owned*. Hence James's old opposition to Harvey. Hence his ambition to get Harvey to punch him on the nose.

'I thought', I say, 'you wanted to get Harvey to punch you on the nose.'

'I did,' he admits. 'But I don't.' He looks at me. 'You think I'm a sell-out?'

Definitely, I think.

'Definitely not,' I say.

James pulls his chair closer. 'Look. All my life I've been picking fights. Every time someone in authority comes near me, I say fuck you fuck you fuck you. It's like . . . it's like *Tourette's Syndrome*. I can't help it. So, along comes the biggest fucking producer in town, the guy everybody's scared of, Godzilla, and he says he wants to offer me a two-picture deal. The point is this. I'm an ant and he's a scorpion.'

'You're an ant?'

'I'm an ant and he's a scorpion. And the ant is the scorpion's worst nightmare. Because the ant runs around the scorpion, round and round, driving him crazy.'

So this is it. James Merendino wants to be an ant. That's why he'll accept a two-picture deal. The fact that a two-picture deal might also be worth something over a million dollars is neither here not there. He wants to be an ant. The fact that he'll also be an extremely *rich* ant is . . . well, it's entirely incidental. Isn't it?

'Isn't it?' I ask.

'Entirely,' he agrees.

Now to brass tacks. A meeting is scheduled with

Harvey's lawyers tomorrow. The man who will broker the deal is my old friend Cassian. Giver Of The $7500 Watch.

'What', I ask, 'if it doesn't work out? Will you fire Cassian?'

'You're goddamn right I will,' James replies. 'But I'll keep the watch.'

Later I ask an industry insider what this all means.

'It means', he says, 'that James is hot.'

'How hot?'

'Hot hot.'

'Hot hot?'

'Hot hot hot.'

'How hot is hot hot hot?'

'Hot hot hot', he says, 'is about as hot as you can get.'

I haven't had a conversation like that since I read *The Cat in the Hat.*

We're having lunch when the phone rings. It's Brian.

BRIAN: Where the hell are you?

ME: Having a massage.

BRIAN: Having a *what?* You're supposed to be with Stephen Loyd for Chrissake!

ME: With Stephen *Loyd?* But I thought you said –

BRIAN: Don't interrupt. Who cares what I said? That was then. This is now. Get your ass over to Stephen. Pronto.

ME: Right. (*Beat*) Er – where is he?

BRIAN: *Where is he?* What kind of director are you? I'll tell you where he is. He's in the fucking *nick!*

Well, not quite. He's actually outside the nick. Apparently, the cops have had enough of Stephen playing Postman Pat up and down the Croisette. Last night they struck. Two truck-loads of them. They took away Stephen's passport, they turned over the van. Now Stephen, Gordon and Spooky are down at the police station. Gordon tried to get the newspapers interested but unfortunately none of their reporters were free. Then he tried to get a TV crew but unfortunately they were all busy. Then he tried to get a lawyer, but unfortunately the only lawyers he could find were all Irish. So now they're on their own.

Stephen meets me outside the police station. He is furious. His face is exactly the colour of tomato ketchup. His neck is a mass of neurasthenic twitchings. Every single blood vessel in his head looks like it's about to explode. 'What the *fuck* are these people scared of?' he yells, thrusting his nose right into my camera lens.

Jesus, I think. I know what they're scared of.

'I haven't a clue,' I say.

'It ain't fucking fair,' he says. 'I mean, you look at *Trainspotting.*'

'*Trainspotting?*'

'*Trainspotting.* A hard-core drugs movie with a lot of jacking up. Right? They come here last year, posters everywhere, have a party, nobody gives a shit. Now we come here with a picture of a bloody cannabis leaf and it's like we're worse than fucking Hitler.'

A policeman comes up to us. 'No cameras! No cameras!' he shouts. In keeping with the great tradition of policemen all over the world, he shoves his hand into the lens.

'We've got to go in,' says Gordon. 'We're gonna fight them.'

'Wait a sec,' I say. Quickly, I get Carl to wire him up for sound. Carl sticks a cleverly concealed radio mike in Gordon's bag. A rapid test. We can hear everything perfectly. Despite the fact that this is technically illegal, I'm not

219

prepared to lose the moment. I've lost too many already. We draw back from the police station, where we can't easily be seen. Stephen, Gordon and Spooky enter the building. I grab a pair of headphones, clamp them over my ears and flick the record button to ON. This is what I hear:

FIRST COP: This is forbidden! This is forbidden! This is forbidden!

GORDON: Show me the law! I want to see the law!

FIRST COP: In France you cannot have this picture.

SECOND COP: We will take away your truck.

FIRST COP: We will take your T-shirts.

SECOND COP: We will take away your posters.

FIRST COP: You listen to me.

GORDON: No, you listen to me.

FIRST COP: No, you listen to me.

GORDON: No, you listen to me.

SECOND COP: (*in French*) Look, shitface, I'm late for my lunch and when I'm late for my lunch I get really fucking angry.

GORDON: What's he talking about?

FIRST COP: He says he hasn't eaten.

SECOND COP: You cannot have this cannabis on your truck. This is the French law.

GORDON: It's not cannabis it's hemp.

FIRST COP: It's cannabis.

GORDON: No, it's not, it's hemp.

FIRST COP: It's cannabis.

GORDON: It's hemp.

FIRST COP: Cannabis.

GORDON: Hemp.

FIRST COP: Cannabis.

GORDON: Hemp.

SECOND COP: Don't fuck with us. If you drive this truck and wear these T-shirts we will arrest you. This is the law.

At this point a policeman spots me. Instantly I whip off the headphones, cut the recording and escape to the crew van round the corner. I feel elated. I'm walking on air. This is terrific stuff. The fact that Stephen, Gordon and Spooky are actually facing arrest, deportation or a 500,000-franc fine doesn't enter my head. For them, this is a disaster. For me, it's . . . a *story!*

3.17 p.m. Stephen, Gordon and Spooky emerge from the police station. It seems they've reached a compromise. They can keep the cannabis leaf if – and only if – they paint a great big red FORBIDDEN sign round it. They have to change this:

INTERDIT!

And if they don't . . . they go to jail.

3.18 p.m. Stephen, Gordon and Spooky discuss the logistics of selling world-wide distribution rights for *Amsterdam* from a police cell.

3.19 p.m. Stephen, Gordon and Spooky decide to buy some paint instead.

3.22 p.m. Gordon gets out his French phrasebook and looks up the words for red paint.

3.27 p.m. Using his French phrasebook, Gordon asks a pedestrian where the nearest paint shop is. The pedestrian points to a place across the street.

3.34 p.m. Using his French phrasebook, Gordon asks the shop assistant for red paint. The shop assistant tries to sell him a bottle of red nail varnish.

3.51 p.m. All the paint shops appear to be closed. Stephen, Gordon and Spooky discuss the logistics of painting the van with red nail varnish. Stephen calculates they will need to buy 637 bottles of red nail varnish to do the job properly.

4.17 p.m. Stephen finds a real paint shop which is open. He buys five tins of red paint.

5.05 p.m. Stephen, Gordon and Spooky begin painting their van directly in front of the Palais, slap bang in the middle of the Croisette.

5.08 p.m. Stephen, Gordon and Spooky succeed in creating the worst traffic jam in the entire history of the Cannes Film Festival.

The chaos is indescribable. Cars are brought to an absolute standstill. Hundreds of people flock to the site. Producers, executives, sales agents, distributors, the pickings of an entire industry, stop to gawk. The Blues Brothers, banging out their music across the street, are completely upstaged. Car-loads of armed police pile into the street, surrounding the van. Walkie-talkies crackle. Sirens scream. Tyres squeal. Horns blast. Photographers and news cameramen rush to the scene. Reporters beg for interviews. Fans beg for autographs. And all the time Stephen, Gordon and Spooky quietly get on with the business of painting a big red cross over the big green

cannabis leaf on their banana-yellow Postman Pat van right
there in the very heart of the very nucleus of the very nub of
the very core of the very kernel of the very epicentre of . . .
the Cannes Film Festival.

Now that is what my Auntie Becky would call chutzpah.

In this one brief moment, these three blokes from
Leytonstone are the hottest story in Cannes. (They're hot
hot hot.) They're the talk of the town. They're the heroes of
the hour. They may be no closer to their £1.2 million. But
boy oh boy, *are they famous!*

And, in the end, isn't that what it's all about?

THURSDAY, 21 MAY, CANNES

Today is D-Day: D-Day for Mike, D-Day for James, D-Day
. . . for me. By the end of today, we will know the answers to
three questions, namely:

(1) Did Mike sell his movie?
(2) Did James get his two-picture deal?
(3) Did I fuck up?

By (3) I mean this: two stories climax today, two ends, two
conclusions. I don't know when or how they're going to
happen. What I do know is this: if my film is to be any good,
if my career is to have a future, if my life is to have a purpose,
I must not miss the moment. Everything hangs on this.

'You do realise', says Brian, 'that everything hangs on this.'

'Yes, Brian.'

'Your film hangs on this.'

'Yes, Brian.'

'Your career.'

'Yes, Brian.'

'Your *life*.'

'Yes, Brian.'

'So do me a favour, will you. Don't fuck up. For once. Just *don't fuck up!*'

'No, Brian.'

The thing which really pisses me off about Brian is that he makes me feel about six.

James is in bed when I get to him.

'Why the hell are you here so early?' he asks.

'I don't want to miss the moment,' I answer.

'Well, you can fuck off,' he says. 'I'm going back to sleep.'

Mike is not in bed when I get to him. He's sitting in a café, drinking black coffee out of a bucket-sized mug. 'I haven't slept for six days,' he says. 'See?' He shows me his hands. They look like several billion bolts have been plugged into them. Apart from my 96-year-old Auntie Becky, I've never seen hands that tremble so much. Mike tries to light another cigarette and almost sets fire to his hair.

'Why are you here so early?' he asks.

'I don't want to miss the moment,' I reply.

'Well,' he says. 'You've come to the right place at the right time.' He points to a bucket full of chalk by his feet. 'I've got my bucket, I've got my chalk, and I've got . . . eight hours.'

'How many seats have you got to fill?'

'A hundred and eighty.'

'How many are you going to fill?'

'Two hundred.' He gets up from the table, grabs up the bucket. 'Right,' he says. 'Let's GO.'

One of the advantages of having several billion volts plugged directly into your nervous system is that you move like . . . *lightning*. Within seconds, Mike is half-way down the street. While we're still fiddling with camera lenses, tripods, microphones, tape recorders, Mike is . . . gone. Disappeared. The moment is being . . . *missed!* What am I going to say to Brian? Quickly, I turn to Dave. Forget the 16mm camera, forget the lenses, mounts, filters, grads, batteries, spare magazines, cans of film, clapper-boards and the rest. Here. Take the video camera. Take a couple of cassettes. And *run*.

Dave is pushing fifty (years, not mph) and running is not something he does every day. But he's a brilliant cameraman and a trooper, and we've been together for years and years, and he likes a challenge, and so he . . . *runs*. He runs after Mike. I run after him. My sound recordist runs after me. Hannah runs after him. My camera assistant runs after her. Everybody chases everybody else madly through the streets of Cannes. We dash round corners, jump past cars, leap over barriers. This is one of those moments when fly-on-the-wall film-making starts to resemble an Olympic Relay Race. Pedestrians eye us curiously. Motorists honk their horns. One or two people even cheer us on.

Somewhere, half-way up the Croisette, Dave finds Mike. Every few seconds, he drops to the ground, whips out a piece of chalk from the bucket, and scrawls over the pavement: SEE TWO BAD MICE, AMBASSADES CINEMA TODAY 7.15 P.M. Sometimes he adds a rider: THE MOVIE WHICH FUCKED GODZILLA. Or: YOUR MOTHER WOULD HATE IT. A few people ask for tickets. Mike dumps armfuls of them in their laps. One hundred and eighty seats. Two hundred to fill. *Christ, he's fast!* The sweat pours off his brow as he hurtles off to the next street, the next block, the next piece of pavement . . . the Great Crazy Olympic Fly-on-the-Wall Relay Race strung out half a mile behind him. Dave, amazingly, keeps up. I get stitches. My blood goes bang bang bang in my temples. I wasn't built for this. I'm too old. I'm too . . . Jesus, I'm thirteen years *younger* than Dave. And look at him. Round and round he circles Mike, the camera constantly moving, a *human Steadicam*, never stopping, never hesitating, the eyepiece stuck like Super-glue to his head. I've got to keep going . . . don't miss the moment . . . whatever I do, don't *fuck up*.

Mike rushes into the garden of the Grand Hotel. We follow. He trips up, the bucket falling to the ground, scattering a thousand pieces of chalk in every direction. Dave is on to it in a flash. I glance up. People sitting at tables, eating breakfast, doing deals. Over there is . . . Christ, *it's James Merendino!* He's supposed to be in bed. He's sitting with his producer. And isn't that . . . isn't that *Cassian?* A glance back to Mike. He's scooping up the chalk, shovelling it into the bucket, moving on. Then back to James, talking to Cassian, discussing . . . the deal. *The deal?* I must not miss the moment. I must not . . . *which moment*, for Christ's sake? They're both having a moment. Mike, James, James, Mike. Everything's happening at once. It's just like my dream. What do I do? Which way do I turn? Bang bang bang goes the blood in my temples. Bang BANG . . .

Somewhere around this point, it appears, I fainted.

A brilliant white light burns the back of my eyeballs. For a moment, the pain is indescribable. Gradually it dulls, deadens into an ache, a rhythmic, beating, slow-burning ache which numbs my eyes, my brain, my mind . . . in the half-consciousness which follows I recognise one thing and one thing only. Exhaustion. A deep, terrible, nerve-sucking,

227

muscle-damping, bone-breaking exhaustion. I open my eyes. Dave is standing over me. So is Hannah, so is Carl. The sky beats down on their heads, a fabulous, impossible blue . . .

'Are you OK?' says Hannah.

'You fainted,' says Dave.

'Just like that,' says Carl. 'Whizz . . . Whee . . . Bang. It was amazingly dramatic.'

For a minute I say nothing. I'm too tired to speak. Then, 'Did we miss . . . *the moment?*' I ask.

'The moment?' says Dave. He smiles. 'The moment . . . is all in the can, baby.'

It takes me a few seconds to realise he's talking about the moment I fainted.

James is sitting in his hotel bedroom, his bare feet stuck on the table, blowing smoke rings in the air. He says, 'Cannes is the worst fucking place for a director in the world. I feel like a cow in a convention of abattoir owners.'

'A cow?' I ask.

'Because it's not about films. It's about money. It's about studio producers hiring the most expensive hookers in town to fuck distributors. The distributors are buying, the producers are selling. This is one equation where the director doesn't fit. Sure, he gets fucked all the time but it's not by hookers.'

'So why are you here?'

'Because I have to be.' James blows another perfect smoke ring into the air.

'You want my advice for any director who wants to come here?' he asks. 'Don't.'

'Don't?'

'Don't. There is no God. Don't come.'

By two o'clock James is getting nervous. Unlike Mike, who has to do pretty much everything himself, James has to do . . . nothing. Except wait. Somewhere, in another hotel, in another part of town, a bunch of people are closeted in a room, dealing, discussing, deliberating his future. He has no say, no influence, no control over his own destiny. Cassian has control, Sam, his producer, has control, Harvey Weinstein has control. But not James. For the next few hours these few people will thrash out the deal, if there is a deal. Meanwhile, James sits in his room and blows smoke rings into the air, and waits. World War Two veterans had an expression for this. They called it sweating out the mission.

4.30 p.m. For the umpteenth time, James looks at his Bulgari platinum-plated $7500 watch. 'Shit,' he says. 'It's stopped.'

Every fifteen minutes or so, in between offering James cigarettes, making sure he's comfortable and dishing out encouraging words, Elizabeth sits on the balcony and makes phone calls. She calls Cassian, she calls Sam, she calls Peter Ward – another producer – she calls Michael Peyser – an executive producer. None of them answers the phone. She leaves message after message and as she does so the tension builds in the room, until it becomes a palpable, physical tension, a tension you can touch, a tension you can *hear*, like somebody scratching his nails on a blackboard. We sit there, filming a little, waiting, finding ourselves suddenly caught up in the drama of the moment, all the while listening to James's stream of jokes, gossip, opinion, anecdotes getting thinner and thinner, and less and less funny, until they finally dry up and stop. Then the phone rings.

CUT TO:

INT. JAMES'S HOTEL BEDROOM. DAY.

Sfx The phone. It's yet another of James's gang of producers on SLC Punk.
*This one is tough and no-nonsense. I have met her once before, on the night of
James's screening. We did not get on.*

ASSOCIATE
(at the end of the phone)

Harvey . . . *scratch* . . . *scratch* . . . meeting . . . *scratch* . . . panic . . .
scratch scratch . . .

JAMES

I'm not panicking . . . I'm not panicking . . . Who's panicking? . . .
Why are you telling me I'm panicking? . . . Do I sound like I'm
panicking? . . . Good-bye.

James switches off the phone. He turns to me.

JAMES

She thinks I'm panicking. Ha ha. That's a fucking joke. She
says, 'James, don't panic, don't panic!' Was I panicking? Ha ha
ha.

He immediately lights up another cigarette.

My relationship with James is a peculiar one. For one thing,
it's curiously competitive. Of course, *I'm* not the one
competing with *him*. But why on earth would he want to
compete with me? What have I got that he hasn't (apart from
a bit of hair)? He's got a movie in Cannes, he's got six movies
behind him, he's got . . . Harvey Weinstein, for God's sake.
I've got a few documentaries, no movie in Cannes and the

230

nearest I ever got to Harvey Weinstein was having a pizza on the Croisette while he was busy giving James bearhugs. I suppose I should be flattered. But I'm not. We spend a lot of our time, James and I, playing Who's The Cleverest Of Them All? We circle round each other, we cut and thrust, we spin out little ironic games to no purpose. Of course, I admire the guy, I like his pluck, his spirit, his chutzpah, but . . . do I really like *him*? I'm pretty certain he doesn't like me.

I sometimes wonder why he agreed to be in this film. Was it vanity? Arrogance? A sense of fun? An opportunity to play the rebel, the punk movie-maker, the guy who creates mayhem and breaks a few legs? I think he's suspicious of me. I think he thinks I intend to take the piss out of him. The truth is, I just want to understand him. For instance: I want to know whether all that stuff about getting Harvey Weinstein to punch him on the nose was actually *true*. Was it just another game or did he actually mean it? And if it was true, if he did mean it, then why is he sitting here now, smoking a hundred Marlboro Lights and panicking about a deal with the very man he once affected to despise? Why is he sticking his head between the lion's jaws? The answer is, I don't know. What I do know is that he's not about to tell me.

6.16 p.m. Everybody pretends not to look at the phone. It sits there on the table, squat and hateful, stubbornly not ringing.

Dave puts the camera down. He says, 'I'm bursting to go to the loo.' He gets up, leaves the room. Nobody looks up. Nobody says anything. Then the phone rings.

Jesus Christ! The moment!

Dave rushes back, picks up the camera. His flies are still undone.

'Cassian,' says James. 'What's up?'

231

Dave fixes focus, trains the lens on James. Everybody holds their breath.

James says, 'Yes . . . No . . . Yes . . . No . . . When? . . . I see . . . Uh-huh . . . OK . . . Right.'

Elizabeth looks at Katrina. Katrina looks at Dave. Dave looks at James. James puts the phone down. He grins. He laughs. 'I've got it,' he says. 'A two-picture deal.'

Everybody screams at once. Katrina hugs him. So does Elizabeth. James's face is bright red. It is an incredibly – and for me a surprisingly – emotional moment. As if all our destinies, mine included, are suddenly bound up with his.

Later, I shake James's hand. 'Congratulations,' I say.

'Thanks,' he replies.

In the space of one phone call, James has just become a millionaire. The deal is worth $1.25 million. What neither of us mentions is that Harvey Weinstein – the man James wanted to provoke into punching him on the nose – is now his boss.

Now it's Mike's turn.

The screening is five hundred yards away, in a street parallel to the Croisette. By the time we get there it's filling up. Mike stands outside, counting heads.

'How many?' I ask.

'Over a hundred,' he says. 'Not enough.'

Peter Johnston is there and so is Rolf. They chat up people in the lobby. In Cassian-speak, they work the crowd. But not Mike. He waits and watches.

'When does the movie start?' I ask.

'In about five minutes.'

'Are you going to watch it?'

'No,' he says. 'It's crap.' He laughs. 'I wouldn't pay to see this piece of shit.'

'You hate it?'

'I love it. But I'm fucking sick of it. I want to kick it out the house.' He glances into the lobby, then back to me. 'I suppose Cannes is as good a place as any to kick it out,' he says.

He looks drained. His fingers are covered in chalk. His hands are still trembling. It's obvious he just wants to be left alone. We go into the lobby, pick up a few shots as the last of the audience shuffles in. One says, '*Two Bad Mice* fucked *Godzilla*. I liked that. That's why I'm here.' He hands Rolf his business card. More business cards. They probably have several suitcases full by now. We retreat to a corner. Mike still waits by the door. Over the PA, somebody announces that the movie is about to start. Just before the doors close, two men, one big and fat, one small and thin, rush into the lobby. It's Stephen and Gordon, come to catch the final performance of *Two Bad Mice*.

We leave Mike in peace. After all, what is there to say? Everybody involved in this story knows what's at stake. Everybody knows that Mike's destiny is bound up with the approval – or disapproval – of the hundred-odd people sitting in this cinema, watching this film. As with James, there's nothing to do but wait. Mike sits down on a bench and counts the minutes. We go to a café down the street and count the minutes there.

Half an hour before the end, we return. Mike is nowhere to be seen. The lobby is empty. From the auditorium, I can hear the muffled soundtrack of the movie. The dull thud of music. A woman's voice shouting. The noise of a car backfiring.

Then Mike appears. 'The fucking projector broke down,' he says.

'What?'

'The fucking projector broke down. About ten minutes ago. The picture just . . . flipped off the screen.'

'Flipped off the screen?'

233

'The guy upstairs', he says, pointing to the projection box, 'is obviously completely stoned.'

I have seen Mike in every conceivable mood: exhilarated, optimistic, pessimistic, elated, depressed, calm and panic-stricken. I have seen him manic, I have seen him angry, I have seen his eyeballs blown half-way out of his skull by a billion volts of pure, unremitting . . . *energy*. But I have never *never* seen him as he is now. What I see is something almost eerily calm, disturbingly quiet, a sort of terrible, final resignation. Maybe I just like the guy, but I too am gutted.

In the run of things, this is unbelievably bad luck. (For us also. After all, we . . . *missed the moment!*) Mike sits down on the stairs. He says, 'Just after that a whole heap of people walked out.'

'How many?'

'God knows. A lot. Too many to count. Maybe . . . twenty or thirty. Maybe forty.'

'Forty?'

For a moment, Mike doesn't answer. Then, in a voice dragged up from somewhere near the floor, he says, 'You know, it was just at the best bit. The bit where everything takes off, where the movie takes on a life of its own. The bit I'm most proud of.'

So this is it. The end of the line. Ten minutes later it's over. A few punters hang around the lobby, making polite conversation. Nobody says let's buy this movie. Nobody says let's do lunch. One man makes a remark about the projector. Mike says, 'The beginning of the film needs to be sharper, I think' and the man nods in agreement. It is the first time I've ever heard Mike apologise for his film. Rolf comes up to Mike, touches him on the shoulder.

Peter arrives with a pizza in a cardboard box. He says, 'Do you want some? I got it from the cheapest place in town.'

At this point I put down the camera. I have no wish to record a ritual of humiliation. No doubt Brian would say I'm missing the moment. But, right now, I couldn't give a fuck about the moment. Of all the people I've followed in Cannes, Mike is the one who touched me the most. And of all of them, perhaps even of Stephen and Gordon, Mike is the one who lost the most.

Somewhere in this diary, I remember saying something about the privilege granted to people who make documentaries. By which I meant the privilege of dropping briefly but somehow intensely into somebody else's life, hopes, dreams, ambitions and failures. Today has been what James Merendino would call a super-concentrated-tomato-paste version of that privilege. Two lives, two film-makers, two stories, two ambitions. Two such different conclusions. Three hours ago I witnessed James make $1.25 million, launching him on the road to fame, glory, success, greater riches. Now I witness . . . this. Mike Hakata isn't going home with anything, except perhaps his pride. What he's going home *to* is the dole. Plus a pile of debts run up by being here. Plus a movie nobody seems to want.

I suppose, in the end, this is what it's all about. This is the astonishing, addictive, roller-coaster-ride experience of making a documentary about Cannes. Because it's all here: success and failure, fame and obscurity, wealth and poverty, glory and humiliation, adoration and ignominy, fantasy and reality, a whole set of oppositions, sometimes comic, sometimes tragic, always fascinating, playing out their consequences in one square mile of one small town in what happens to be the biggest film festival of the world.

Oh, and by the way, Stephen and Gordon *loved* the movie. And we all know what that means.

ACT III

Finale

Two days later Mike left Cannes for good. I saw him only twice. Once on the day after the screening and once when he took the bus to the airport. The day after the screening he was back in his office, on the phone. By now, he'd run out of money, which meant he'd run out of the key staples of survival: cigarettes, black coffee and phone cards. With the very last of his phone cards he was trying to call those few distributors who had stayed to watch his film. Some of them weren't in. Some of them were engaged. Some of them had already left town. None of them called back. In the end he hung up. He said, 'I'm fucking sick of this phone.' Then he took down the sign which said TWO BAD MICE OFFICE. THIS IS NOT A PUBLIC PHONE, stuffed it in his pocket and walked away. When I next saw the phone box, a few hours later, somebody else was in it. Just another public phone on the Croisette. There was nothing to suggest it had ever been anything else.

The second, and last, time I saw Mike was the following day, at the bus station. He was on his own. Rolf and Peter had already left. He had his bags, an old suitcase and his six red cans of film. He dumped the cans in the luggage compartment. 'Well,' he said. 'I suppose that's it then.'

'That's it,' I said.

'It's been . . . fun.'

'Fun, yes,' I said.

We wait for the bus to start. A man closes the luggage door,

239

locking the bags, the suitcase and the six red cans inside. 'You'd better get in,' I say. 'Don't want to miss your flight.'

'No.' For a moment, neither of us speaks. 'Well,' he says. 'Be seeing you.'

'Good luck, Mike.'

'Good luck to you.' He climbs into the bus. 'Who knows?' he says. 'Maybe I'll be back next year?'

'Who knows?' I say. 'Maybe you will.'

We film the bus leaving for the airport. It disappears down the Croisette, past the Carlton, past the Majestic, past the phone box, past the Palais, until it's lost in the haze and the traffic.

We wander back through the bus station, out into the streets. It's a hot Saturday afternoon. The Festival ends tomorrow. The city is visibly emptier, the shops, cafés and bars less crowded. We stop by a stall on the Croisette for a drink. On the pavement, I notice a scrawl of chalk marks, already fading in the sun. TWO BAD MICE FUCKED GODZILLA. This is all that's left of Mike and his movie.

And yet . . . perhaps it's appropriate. Last night, *Godzilla* was screened in the Palais. Everybody hated it. The critics panned it. Most people thought it was the worst movie in Cannes. TWO BAD MICE FUCKED GODZILLA?

In the end, maybe it did.

'I am *Goliath*,' says James Merendino, the day after he became a millionaire.

'Why are you Goliath?'

'Because', says James, 'I own the world.' And he blows an exhaustful of smoke straight into the camera lens.

Something has happened to James. Well, *of course* something has happened to James. He's a millionaire – or about to be. He's got a two-picture deal. He's got the most

240

famous – and the most infamous – boss in the history of movies since Louis B. Mayer. He's . . . *in the Club*. All this is perfectly true, but it's not quite what I mean. What I mean is this: success has changed him overnight. He's a different person. He's cockier, brasher, more confident, more arrogant, more egotistical. The power relationship between us has subtly changed. Collusion has been replaced by concession. Suddenly, I'm the lucky guy who gets an interview with Goliath. This is apparent from the moment I meet him in the Grand Hotel. He says, 'I can only give you half an hour.'

'What do you mean, half an hour?'

'Half an hour. That's all I've got. I've got a meeting with my agent. I've got a meeting with Miramax. I've got meetings with my lawyers. I've got meetings with my producers. You'd better set up quickly.'

So we set up quickly.

Years ago, when I started training, the BBC used to show a video to budding directors. It was called 'How Not to Direct'. It contained bucket-loads of advice about how not to do things. How not to frame a shot, how not to cut across eyelines, how not to mix up wide-angles and close-ups . . . a whole gamut of sins never to be committed. The worst of these was the Flower-Pot Shot. The Flower-Pot Shot is the shot so framed that a flower-pot appears to be growing out of an interviewee's head. It looks ridiculous. Studies have revealed that it's virtually impossible to take anyone remotely seriously when a flower-pot is growing out of their head. I decide now to enact my own personal variation of the Flower-Pot Shot called . . . the 'Giant Palm Tree Shot'. In this instance, a conveniently placed palm tree appears to be growing out of the interviewee's head. The interviewee, of course, is James.

I know this is juvenile. But I'm cross. And probably

jealous. And fed up with James. So we set up the shot (we've only got *half an hour*) and stick James in a chair twenty yards in front of the biggest palm tree in the gardens, and there he is, James Merendino, the world's newest greatest director, the hottest talent at Miramax, Harvey Weinstein's personal baby, the next Tarantino . . . with a giant palm tree growing straight out of his head. My cameraman checks the frame and starts to giggle. The amazing thing is that James doesn't notice. 'Remember,' he says, 'how I wanted to get Harvey to punch me? Well, he did – he punched me with a contract.'

'So it's *Harvey* now.'

'Yeah, it's Harvey. We're on first-name terms. You know what he said to me last night? He said, look kid, you don't have to worry about a thing now, you've paid your dues, you're rich, you're famous, we're gonna be making movies together . . . you own *the world*.' He raises his glass to the camera. 'I guess bigger is better,' he says.

'I guess,' I agree.

'How much time have we got left?' asks James.

'Ten minutes.'

'Ten minutes. Elizabeth, cigarette.'

James sits coiled up in his seat. The energy burns off him. I have never seen him quite like this. It's as if every trait has been somehow magnified, blown up, enlarged to Goliath-sized proportions. For instance, he always spoke fast. Now he speaks . . . faster. The words blast out like bursts of machine-gun fire, a crazy, adrenalin-powered, hyper-speeded eruption of innuendo, metaphor, paradox, hyperbole . . . until my head spins with his and I no longer know who or what he is. Is it all a game? Or is this the 'real' James: a monster-sized ego, once hidden, now suddenly – and shockingly – laid bare by the catalyst of success?

'You see how things *turn*?' says James.

242

'I do.'

'Things just turn, you know. And I guess the audience is saying right now, are you a sell-out? Well, here's what I say to the audience.' He raises his glass again. 'My father told me a story when I was a kid and I guess he got it from *The Godfather* but I didn't know that at the time, so I thought my father was a very clever man. He said, "Keep your friends close, but your enemies closer . . . And keep film-makers *up your ass*." '

He laughs. So do I. Neither of us means it.

I have one final question: 'What's your next project?'

'My next project?' James leans forward, blows another exhaustful of smoke into the lens. 'My next project . . . is a documentary about film-makers taking their films to the Cannes Film Festival.'

'What's it going to be like?'

'It's going to be a whole lot fucking better than yours,' says James.

Later, I meet Cassian on the terrace of his hotel.

'So now you and James are friends again,' I say.

'Oh yeah, well,' he says, 'we're never not friends.'

'He's not going to fire you then.'

'Ha ha ha,' says Cassian. 'Look, it's all bravado, it's all an act, the guy is just a total actor, he's a total movie star, he's unbelievable, everything he does is some sort of act he's pulling on you, he's the smartest guy I've ever met, he's . . .'

While Cassian continues in this vein, I am suddenly tempted to tell him he has a piece of sausage on his face.

But I never do.

This evening, James is invited to a party at the Hotel du Cap, the most expensive hotel in Cannes. The party is given by his agency, William Morris. The du Cap, an elegant eighteenth-century mansion on the outskirts of Cannes, sits in perfectly manicured gardens sweeping down to a private beach. It oozes privilege, wealth, exclusion. We, of course, have long been denied permission to film there. The hotel is out of bounds, the grounds are out of bounds . . . the party is out of bounds. But we go anyway.

We take the transit van up the winding roads and into the hills beyond the town. The du Cap prides itself on being apart, a distinct, hermetically sealed oasis amid the frenzy of the Festival. Huge ornamental gates divide the hotel from the street. Remote TV cameras keep a watchful eye on anything that moves. The place is somehow reminiscent of a very exclusive lunatic asylum, designed as much to keep the residents in as members of the public out. Normally, things are very quiet here. The odd car enters or exits, the electric gates swing open and shut, the cameras turn slowly on their mounts, ever watching, guarding, protecting . . . But not tonight. Tonight is party night and the street outside the hotel is packed with limos disgorging guests. We take up position a few yards away.

Some of the guests I recognise. A few I met in LA weeks ago, others in London, some here in Cannes. Almost all of them are players, the movers and shakers of the business, the great and the good, occasionally the famous. They've come to mingle and gossip, and swap stories on the last weekend of the Festival. It's a world away from Mike Hakata and his six cans of film, from Stephen and Gordon on their camp site. What we have here is a living, breathing definition of the Club, a tiny élite of men and women who run one of the most powerful industries in the world. A world of Goliaths and no Davids.

A few moments later a car pulls up. James gets out. With him are Elizabeth and Katrina. From the other side of the street I watch. He enters the hotel. He looks confident, he looks good, he looks . . . *the business*. This is now his world. He has the patronage of Harvey Weinstein. (And nobody fucks with Harvey Weinstein.) He's in the Club. Yesterday, he was threatening to get Harvey to punch him on the nose. Tonight, they'll be discussing golf strokes. Such, I suppose, is the meaning of success.

As for me, I feel . . . what do I feel? Am I jealous of James? Is this what *I* want too? A limo, a fabulous hotel, a glittering cocktail party on the most exclusive terrace of one of the most exclusive hotels in the world? Of course I do. Who on earth wouldn't? And yet . . . there's something else which disturbs me. And that something else is James himself. It's not just his cockiness, nor his conceit, but the sense that somehow all these things are the price of his success. Is this what happens when David becomes Goliath? Or is it what happens when *this* David becomes *this* Goliath? I wish I knew.

The moment passes. Dave puts away the camera. We pile the equipment into the van. I get in the front, the rest of the crew are in the back. I start the engine and we slide past the gates of the hotel, past the TV cameras, past the security guards, past the last few knots of guests waiting to enter, past a huge balding bloke in a suit stepping out of a limo . . . *Harvey Weinstein?*

The moment! Quick, jam on the brakes! The van squeals to a halt . . . I grab the camera, leap out of the van . . . Dave leaps out after me . . . Carl leaps out after *him* . . . Harvey—*is it Harvey?*—turns round, glances across the road . . . Dave fumbles with the camera . . . come on, *come on* . . . the man steps through the gates . . . and is gone.

He's gone. And we missed it. (Again!) A couple of heavy-duty guys bar all access beyond the gates. I consider whether to film them, but decide not to. They don't look too friendly. They don't look friendly at all. After all, *nobody fucks with Harvey Weinstein.* Not us. Not them. Not the guests inside.

And certainly not James Merendino. Not now.

The last few days before the end of the Festival are difficult for Erick Zonca. To be odds-on favourite for the *Palme d'Or* is bound to raise the temperature a few degrees, to wind up one or two nerves, to add a little tension. Not that I know this first-hand, of course. He won't talk to me. Pascale grabs bits of him when she can – which is almost never – and he dutifully parades himself in all the places where odds-on *Palme d'Or* favourites are expected to parade themselves. Mostly, he does interviews, an average of forty a day, repeating the same things over and over again until a sort of numbed exhaustion sets in. This has its advantages, since it must be difficult to care about *anything*, even winning the *Palme d'Or*, when you're this numb and this exhausted. Meanwhile, Pascale does her best and I forget all about Erick Zonca and his movie, and his prospects and the fact that we might actually have hit upon the biggest and most remarkable of all our stories bar none.

Bar none. Consider this. A couple of days ago, Harvey Weinstein invited Erick Zonca to discuss his movie. A meeting was arranged. At the appointed hour the Miramax lawyers turned up. So did Zonca's producer. So did Zonca's distributor. So did everyone. The only person who didn't turn up was Zonca. And the reason why Zonca didn't turn up was because . . . he wasn't there. There was some confusion about timings. Zonca went to see a movie instead. Now this is something nobody does, *ever*. When Harvey whistles, you come. You don't *not turn up*. Did James Merendino not turn up? No. Does Quentin Tarantino not turn up? He does not. So what does this say about Erick Zonca?

(1) That only someone with a movie tipped for the *Palme d'Or* can do this sort of thing and still get away with it.

(2) That the rumour now is that Harvey Weinstein wants to offer Erick Zonca a 26-picture deal. This is known in the trade as the Spurned Lover Syndrome.

(3) That therefore Zonca is by far the most remarkable of our stories. Bar none. Compared with him, James Merendino is a minnow. (Or an ant.)

Sunday night is prize-giving night, the last gasp of the Festival. The ceremony takes place in the 2400-seat cinema in the Palais. The obvious parallel is Oscar night, but there are key differences. First, people very rarely win more than one prize. Multiple winners are virtually unknown. If you get the Special Jury Prize you're unlikely to get the *Palme d'Or*. Second, you always know you've won something *in advance*. What you don't know is what you've won. If this seems a little perverse, consider the problems. Cannes is an expensive place. Nobody wants to stay longer than they have to. And nobody wants to stay, only to discover they haven't won a thing. So the jury makes things easier. They tell people. Not explicitly, though. They say, 'We think, you know, it might be a good idea if maybe you didn't leave Cannes *just yet*, and you know that means you've won a prize. On the night, you find out whether what you've won is Best Location Sound* or the *Palme d'Or*. Some people call that pragmatism. Others call it sadism.

For the last twenty-four hours the jury is closeted in some undisclosed hotel in order to decide who wins what.

---

* Actually, there's no such thing.

Like any jury, they eat together, they sleep together, they sit and talk and argue and horse-trade, they get sick of the sight of each other . . . but they don't stop until they're done. Like the election of a new Pope, these deliberations are steeped in the most extraordinary secrecy. And all the time, while they're at it, *long before* they're at it, the rumour mills grind, the pundits pontificate, the fans place their bets, the gendarmes polish their boots, the red carpet is swept, hoovered and dusted, and the film-makers . . . do more interviews.

By Saturday afternoon, the big money for the *Palme d'Or* is on three candidates: Angelopoulos, Benigni and Zonca. By Sunday morning, Zonca is *hors de combat*. He hides in his room, switches off the phone, sticks a DO NOT DISTURB sign outside the door and . . . goes to sleep. Nobody can reach him, not his producer, not his distributor, not his press agent and definitely not Pascale. And while he sleeps, or tries to sleep, or turns and twists in his bed and stares at the ceiling or does whatever it is you do when you're a once-obscure first-time director with a movie tipped for the most prestigious movie prize in the world, the jury, led by Martin Scorsese, reach their conclusions. The Pope is elected.

Somewhere around this point, we are up in the hills in a villa. The villa is owned by Zonca's distributor, a flamboyant man with an expensive taste in suits. He's become something of an ally (which means I'm actually allowed in the villa). I spend the time filming, and waiting, and watching, and waiting, and filming, while the distributor and the producer and the press agent and a whole host of other people intimately connected to Zonca's fortunes deliberate his chances, and his future, without him. They sit by the swimming pool, they drink excellent wine, they smoke Gauloises, and all the while the city hums below them, the rumours spin, the punters take their bets and Erick Zonca stares at the ceiling . . .

Back at the villa the phone rings. Zonca's producer takes the call. 'We think it would be a good idea if you didn't leave Cannes *just yet.*' What does it mean? Which prize has he won? Is it the *Palme d'Or*? Is it the Special Jury Prize? (Is it Best Location Sound?) Who's going to tell him? More to the point, *where is he?* The distributor tries his hotel. The hotel tries his room. The phone rings and rings and rings . . . and then Zonca answers it. At this point the distributor demonstrates his peculiar sense of humour by telling Zonca he's awfully sorry but unfortunately he hasn't won any prize at all. Everybody thinks this is hilarious (except Zonca who thinks it's true) until they finally take pity, tell him about the phone call and order him to get the hell up here, to the villa. Which, within the hour, he does.

By six o'clock, Zonca waits with his entourage for the car which will take him to the Palais. At this point, I should explain my state of mind. Stripped to essentials, my state of mind is this: what is *his* state of mind? Since I'm not allowed to ask him (I'm not allowed *near* him) I hit on the idea of fixing a remote video camera in his car. While Zonca sits in the lobby of the Martinez Hotel, my cameraman sticks the little video device on the dashboard of his car, pointing straight at the back seat. We do a quick test . . . it works. It's *beautiful*. Now, at last, we will witness Zonca's every reaction, every gesture, every word, every last trace of emotion as it crosses his face. This, I should add, isn't done on the sly. Not at all. Zonca's producer knows, his distributor knows, his press agent knows, his driver knows, everybody knows . . . except Zonca. I thought they were going to tell him. They thought I was going to tell him. As a result, nobody told him. In a few moments he is about to find out.

CUT TO:

INT. ZONCA'S CAR. TWENTY MINUTES BEFORE
THE CEREMONY.

Zonca enters the car with his two actresses. They all huddle in the back. The chauffeur gets in the front. For the next few minutes Zonca can relax, away from the glare of cameras. Except he can't because our camera is pointing directly at him.

Just as the car starts to move, Zonca and his two actresses suddenly notice the camera. They stare and stare and stare at it. They are speechless.

> ZONCA
> (*in French*)
What the bloody hell is that?

> DRIVER
It's a camera.

> ZONCA
> (*Who is tipped to win the* Palme D'Or *and knows what a camera looks like*)
What the hell is it doing in my car?

> DRIVER
It's the BBC.

> ZONCA
The *what?*

DRIVER

The BBC. You see they're doing this very interesting
documentary about first-time directors who are tipped to win
the *Palme d'*. . .

ZONCA

I know all that. Get rid of it.

DRIVER

Get rid of it?

ZONCA
(*he is absolutely furious*)

Get rid of it! *Now!*

*The driver twists the camera round, rips it off its mount and chucks it on the
floor. Amazingly, it keeps running. This means that instead of getting exclusive
shots of Erick sweating his guts out ten minutes before the biggest moment of his
entire career, we get exclusive shots of the driver's feet.*

Well, it was worth a try – and, I suppose, predictable. And I'm
not sure whether we would have got that much, anyway. Zonca
is not the man to show his emotions. Whatever he may feel, he
doesn't reveal it. Not to us. Not to his actresses. I suspect not
even to his friends. That's just the sort of guy he is.

Access to the ceremony is a bit like travelling by air. First class
is the 2400-seat Palais theatre itself. This is where all the
nominees sit. It's where all the grandees of the industry sit.
(It's also where Harvey Weinstein sits.) Business class is the
Debussy theatre, also in the Palais, where the ceremony is
projected live on to a screen. This is where I am. Economy is
everywhere else (i.e. outside). This is where the masses are, the
thousands of fans who stand in the cold and watch the whole

thing on a giant TV screen. Since Alan is banned from the Palais for the rest of his natural life, we stick him in Economy.

At seven o'clock the event begins. From where I stand in the Debussy theatre, I can watch it on the screen. I can also hear the real thing outside. The noise is terrific. The shouts, the cheers, the music . . . I hear it all in stereo. Outside, the first cars are pulling up, doors are opened, famous faces spill out on to the red carpet, pose for the cameras, for the photographers, for the thousands of fans, move on . . . *look*, there's John Travolta! . . . there's Bruce Willis! . . . there's my old friend Claudia Schiffer! Up on the screen, we get a grandstand view, the sweep of the red carpet, the grand panorama of crowds and cars and cops, the celebrities trooping up the steps, to the seat of the gods . . . to the Palais itself. They come singly, they come in groups and the long line of limos stretches half-way down the Croisette, inching forward through the crowds . . . Somewhere in there is Zonca's car, and Zonca, and his actresses, and my camera . . . *My camera!* Think of the shots I'm getting right now! The fear! The excitement! The anticipation! The *moment!* . . . Of course the only moment I'm actually getting is a ten-minute shot of the driver's feet, but I don't know this, not now, and a wave of excitement, a thrill of thrills, whips through me because I know we're near the climax to my film, the point where the hero faces the greatest test of his life, and the audience, every one of them, is on the edge of their seats, just as I am now . . . And then at last he arrives and the car doors are opened, and there he is, Erick Zonca, first-time film-maker, tipped for the *Palme d'Or*, snatched from obscurity into fame, from darkness into the limelight . . . once David, now Goliath, verily a King of Cannes. A huge cheer goes up.

Fifteen minutes later the doors are shut, the audience is seated, a great hush settles on the fans outside. The prize giving begins. Zonca is about eight rows from the front. His two lead actresses are on his right. Virginie, his co-writer, is on his left. On the stage, a woman announces the prizes. Martin Scorsese announces the prize winners. He wears bifocals, he speaks lousy French and he looks for all the world like a crotchety old headmaster. This is entirely appropriate since the ceremony itself closely resembles a school prize giving, at least the kind that I remember. At any moment I expect Scorsese to announce the winner for Best History Essay or Best Science Project. Like any school prize giving (like my school prize giving) everything is surprisingly amateurish. Announcers fumble their lines, prize winners fumble *their* lines, and the whole thing is punctuated by those odd, uncomfortable pauses which make everyone feel . . . odd and uncomfortable. This is a world away from the slick operation of, say, the Oscars. In a way, I find it rather endearing. I always liked prize giving.

And yet . . . there is tension. One by one, the prizes are announced. The small ones first (e.g. Best Short), then the bigger ones. The ones we're all waiting for. Whatever I think about Erick Zonca, I am suddenly bound up in his fate. After all, his fate affects my fate. If he wins, I've got an end, a denouement. I go out with a bang. So I sit in the Debussy theatre, and watch Scorsese screw up his French verbs and the prize winners go up to the stage, collect their prizes (do they say Sir?) and tumble back to their seats amidst thunderous applause . . . And still Zonca's name isn't mentioned, still he isn't chosen.

One by one the winners come on to the stage . . . Now we're on to the Special Jury Prize. Scorsese opens the envelope, adjusts his bifocals, looks up to the audience, to Zonca, to me and announces . . . 'Roberto Benigni for *La Vita è Bella*.' This brings the house down, not least because Benigni (whose French is also lousy) appears to think he's just won

253

the *Palme d'Or* and proceeds to kiss every single member of the jury before throwing himself at Scorsese's feet and kissing his shoes. He is the hero of the hour. Everybody claps and laughs and claps again, and Benigni bows and waves, and is utterly, enchantingly overwhelmed by the occasion, with his hair sticking up like a clown and his face like an Italian Woody Allen . . . and I'm sitting there thinking why oh why didn't we go for *him* instead?

And now Scorsese announces the prize for Best Actress, and the same ritual is repeated, the same bifocal-adjustment routine, the same opening of the envelope, the same hushed expectation. Scorsese leans towards the microphone. *And the winners are* . . . Elodie Bouchez and Natacha Régnier for *La Vie Revée des Anges*. It takes me a second to grasp that this is Zonca's movie. It takes me another to understand that this means he hasn't won the *Palme d'Or*.

He hasn't won the *Palme d'Or*. Not until that moment do I realise just how much I wanted him to win. I really wanted him to win. Later, watching a tape of the ceremony, I look closely at him, searching for signs of − of what? Disappointment? Failure? Defeat? Rejection? Several times I rewind the tape, scrutinising his face, analysing his features, as if somehow I want him to be what I think he ought to be. But he's not. He claps, he laughs, he kisses the two actresses, he cheers, and there is something in his eyes, in his whole expression, which I find extraordinarily moving. Perhaps it sounds silly, but to me it looks like love.

The *Palme d'Or* went to Angelopoulos. But I didn't wait to see it. By then, I'd already left.

There are people whose intimacies are open from the start, who invite you into their deepest desires, their fears, loves ambitions, dreams. And there are people who don't. Zonca is

254

one of these. The irony is, I never saw it. What I saw was a man who just didn't want to be in my film. I saw a personal affront. Only on this last night, in this last moment, did I recognise the man for what he really is. It made me feel cheap.

Zonca left the Palais after the ceremony. Not to fanfares and trumpets, far from it. He left with his friends, his producer, his distributor, his two actresses and Virginie. I saw them cross the street. There were no cameras, no paparazzi, no cheers. He wasn't tipped for the *Palme d'Or* now. I watched him disappear into the crowds, unrecognised. Once, he looked round. Possibly he saw me. But I don't think so. I think he was looking at the Palais. Perhaps he was wondering if he'd ever be back.

Up at the camp site, Stephen Loyd is in trouble. He's lost his tin opener. Given the fact that absolutely everything he eats comes out of a tin, this is a major crisis. For the next five minutes Spooky bashes a tin of sardines with a hammer, until the stuff suddenly squirts all over his face. Then he does the same with a tin of baked beans. Then he mixes the two together on a plastic plate. Breakfast is ready. We're not hungry.

This is their last day in Cannes. They leave tomorrow. Despite the fact that nobody has bought the script, they are happy. For one thing, everybody knows who they are. Stephen shows me an article in *Screen International* which is all about . . . Stephen. He's been on French national TV. He's been interviewed on the radio. He's been courted by the papers. He's made *an impact*. The consequences of all this publicity are twofold: (a) Spooky and Gordon are sick of the sight of him and (b) he's losing his voice.

'With a bit of luck,' says Spooky, 'he'll never find it again.'

So this is it. The adventure is over. In a couple of days they'll all be back in Leytonstone, Stephen in his minicab, Gordon in his cutting room, Spooky on the dole. And Cannes will seem like a dream. I drive them into town for one last interview. We stop outside the Majestic Hotel. The barriers are still up, but there are fewer fans and fewer paparazzi. The lobby is full of suitcases. The film people are leaving. Tomorrow, the dentists will arrive.

We set up by the swimming pool. The light dances on the water. It is a lovely morning. On the terrace a few late risers are eating breakfast. White-jacketed waiters hover over tables. They're not serving sardines.

'Well,' I say, 'this is it.'

'This is it,' says Gordon.

'Thank God,' says Stephen. 'I'm shattered.'

'What do you think you've achieved?'

'Well . . . we nearly got arrested,' says Gordon.

'And we're in all the papers,' says Stephen.

'And on telly,' says Gordon.

'Well, I am,' says Stephen. 'You're not.'

'But we're not going home with a cheque,' says Gordon.

'We're not,' says Stephen. 'But we had some good meetings. Like with that Wendy Mango person.'

'Wendy Streich.'

'Who?'

'Wendy Streich. And it's Manga Films. And you fucked it up.'

'Who fucked it up?'

'You did.'

'No, I didn't.'

'Yes, you did.'

'No, I didn't.'

'Yes, you did.'

Oh, God, not again. For a moment I think they're going to have a fight, right here, in the middle of the Majestic Hotel.

I change the subject. 'Has it been worth it?'

Stephen ponders. 'We could have done better.'

'We definitely could have done better,' Gordon agrees.

'But you know what they say,' says Stephen. 'It ain't over till the fat lady sings.'

Behind them, the late risers have left. Waiters begin to lay tables for lunch. A palm tree sways gently in the breeze. Somebody dives into the pool.

'I dunno,' says Stephen. 'It was a lot better than driving a fucking minicab for two weeks.'

'I'll second that,' says Gordon.

And they both start to laugh.

Tonight, their last night, Stephen, Gordon and Spooky go to a party. Not any old party, but a glamorous, glittering, star-studded party on a private beach opposite the Carlton. It's Spooky's birthday and we want to give them all a treat. Pascale has got the invites, Brian has hired the dinner-jackets. Up at the camp site the three of them get togged up. Despite the fact that Stephen wears his flip-flops, he looks the business. They all do. As they pose for a photo, I can't help thinking that even if they didn't get their £1.2 million, at least they got to wear the suits.

Later, at the party, I catch up with them. Salsa music blares out over the beach, over the sea, over the yachts anchored in the bay. Roman Polanski is here, John Hurt is here, there are scores of beautiful women. Couples dance under the pavilion. Everyone drinks champagne. Tomorrow some of the yachts will go to Monte Carlo for the Grand Prix. The stars will go home. The news crews will pack up. The posters will come down. This pavilion, like all the others, will be dismantled. Within hours there will be nothing to suggest the Festival ever existed. It will be as if it never was. And Cannes, once more, will revert to what it always was: a sleepy, out-of-season town on the sleepy, out-of-season Riviera. Until next year.

I leave Spooky and Gordon sitting at the bar, and wander off to the beach. Stephen is standing there, alone. He looks out at the yachts. A huge liner, the *Normandie*, squats on the horizon, brilliantly lit. A couple of naked girls cavort in the sea. The music thuds behind us. Somewhere in the distance, fireworks light up the sky. For several minutes we stand together, taking in the view. Neither of us speaks. Then Stephen turns to me. He is smiling. 'This is the business,' he says. 'This is what it's all about.'

Perhaps, in the end, he's right. I suppose their chances of raising £1.2 million were a little . . . optimistic? But maybe that's missing the point. After all, they tried. They got here. And they made their mark. That's more than most people do. It is something to drive a minicab in Leytonstone one minute, and rub shoulders with Roman Polanski the next.

'I'll be back next year,' Stephen says. 'And when I do I'll bring my yacht. And I'll dump it in the middle of the harbour and stick a forty-foot spliff leaf on the side. And I'll have the biggest party in Cannes.' He chuckles. 'And Bruce Willis will be there.'

And I hope he will.

Some time around dawn I leave the party. The Croisette is almost deserted. A couple of revellers make their way back to their hotels. An old man sweeps the side of the road. The sun touches the tops of the hills. Another golden morning in Cannes. I walk past the Palais. It is empty. Nothing moves, nothing stirs. Flags hang limp in the still air. The red carpet stretches up the stairs. Tomorrow it will be rolled up, put away for another year. The dentists won't be needing it.

It is the end of the road – for Cannes, for my characters, for me. Over the next twelve weeks I will sit in a windowless room, surrounded by half a million feet of film, and attempt to make sense of this adventure. I will try to contain so many hundreds of moments, so many dozens of stories, into one seamless ninety-minute spectacle. The thought appals me. As if life is ever really like that. As if that's how things really were.

But that's all in the future. This is now. And now . . . there's nothing to do. There's nobody to film. There's no-where to go except home. Suddenly, I am free. I suppose I should be exhilarated. But I'm not. If anything, I feel a little sad.

I turn up the street to my hotel. The receptionist is asleep, and I get the key myself. I go up to my room, open the door. I'm too tired to undress, too tired even to take off my shoes. I fall on to the bed, shut my eyes, and sink into the longest, deepest sleep I have had in five months. This time, not even Brian wakes me up.

POSTSCRIPT

In February 1999, Mike Hakata took *Two Bad Mice* to the Saarbrücken Film Festival, along with a year's supply of chalk. Despite an animated campaign, nobody bought it. Never one to be beaten, he has since re-edited the movie for the fifth – and, he swears, final – time. A couple of distributors are said to be interested. Meanwhile, he has written several new scripts, none of which has proposed budgets of less than £100.

Since Cannes, Erick Zonca has gone from strength to strength. *La Vie Revée des Anges* won critical acclaim all over the world, winning two Césars in France and a host of other awards. It was also nominated for an Oscar in the Best Foreign Film category. It didn't win. Benigni got the Oscar instead.

James Merendino's movie, *SLC Punk*, opened the Sundance Film Festival in January 1999. Despite his penchant for calling me at three o'clock in the morning, we still remain friends. To date, he has not fired his agent.

Stephen, Gordon and Spooky got as far as Lyon before the van broke down. It was still there three months later. Stephen plans to turn it into a museum if his movie is ever made.

*

After four months and several cardiac scares, I finally finished the documentary, *Waiting for Harvey*. Then I began writing this book. Now I'm waiting for Harvey Weinstein to buy the rights so I can make the movie of the book of the movie. Who knows? Maybe I'll take it to Cannes?

On 10 January 1999 my Auntie Becky died, aged 97. She never saw the movie.

ABOUT THE AUTHOR

Stephen Walker was born in London in 1961. He spent ten years at the BBC, first as a researcher and subsequently as a director, making films on subjects as diverse as the Battle of the Somme, the history of toys and a Jewish wedding. He also directed *Prisoners In Time*, a drama starring John Hurt, in which a former British POW confronts his Japanese torturer fifty years after the war. He lives in London with his wife and eight-year-old daughter.